WAKE ME

When It's Time to Work

Cashman Dudley
An imprint of Gulf Publishing Company
Houston, Texas

WAKE ME

When It's Time to Work

Surviving Meetings, Office Games, and the People Who Love Them

T. R. EDEL

WAKE ME
When It's Time to Work

Copyright ©1999 by Gulf Publishing Company, Houston, Texas. All rights reserved. This book, or parts thereof, may not be reproduced in any form without express written permission of the publisher.

Cashman Dudley
An imprint of Gulf Publishing Company
Book Division
P.O. Box 2608 □ Houston, Texas 77252-2608

10 9 8 7 6 5 4 3 2 1

Library of Congress Cataloging-in-Publication Data
Edel, T. R.
    Wake me when it's time to work : surviving meetings, office games, and the people who love them / T.R. Edel.
       p.   cm.
    Includes index.
    ISBN 0-88415-227-8 (alk. paper)
    1. Office politics.   I. Title.
HF5386.5.E34   1999
650.1′3—dc21   99-22351
                                             CIP

Printed in the United States of America.

Printed on acid free paper (∞).

To the idealists, so they may

understand more of life

before it happens

Contents

Inside the Company, *or* *And You Thought Only People Could Get Indigestion*

The Mistreatment of Employees, *or* *What the Company Giveth, the Company Can Taketh Away*

Closing Remarks, *or* *Either Use Your Noggin or Take a Floggin'*

Index

Introduction

~ or ~

Leave Your Idealism at the Office Door

I wrote this book to provide my grown children, as they prepared to enter the work force, with an understanding of the happenings that occur in large companies. I hoped this information would help them, as employees, to better appreciate the real reasons things work the way they do. Now that they are both successful business people, I'd like to share these perspectives with you.

Management neither officially recognizes nor writes down the insights contained in this book; rather this information evolved over time and is usually only apparent to the seasoned veteran. Misinformation, specious perceptions, and the like are all fostered by the people in power to sustain their positions and to maintain the illusion that everything will work out. To such people, the good of the company becomes secondary while the majority of workers suffer the consequences of such behavior. To survive and to maintain your sense of purpose within any large organization, you should become familiar with the topics discussed in this invaluable employee guide.

I concentrated on the *darker side* of corporate life to enlighten the idealist. Company personalities, games, meetings, procedures, management, and so on are described with a dose of sarcasm to remove any false illusions associated with employment in a large corporation. By recognizing the reasons behind what is going on, you can better cope with anomalies that would otherwise frustrate a thinking being. I inserted humor where appropriate, but the more serious subjects are presented from the vantage point of employees who directly or indirectly experienced these scenarios. My desire is that telling it like it is will expose the false impressions that organizations and people perpetuate to suit their own needs and goals.

T. R. Edel

Corporate Culture Shift

~ or ~

If You Want a Best Friend Get a Dog, Not a Job

In previous decades successful corporations learned that happy workers contributed more than unhappy workers. These companies made their employees feel they were somehow special and, above all, appreciated. In recent times, companies experiencing some financial duress have been willing to compromise this attitude. Read on and learn more about how the modern corporation treats its employees.

It benefits companies to foster the notion that the primary policy toward their employees is respect for the individual or even the idea that their greatest asset is their employees. Furthermore, companies publicize the perception that all employer/employee relationships stem from these beliefs.

Now exactly how does such a statement affect the employee? First, it makes people feel like the company really cares about them, so they go the extra mile when asked to work overtime, even for periods of several years, because they believe the company will always do the right thing. (Note that for salaried workers most overtime is unpaid.) People tolerate excessive travel, late night meetings, weekend work, and so on because they want to believe the company really appreciates their efforts. Fostering this work ethic clearly benefits the company because employees unknowingly buy into this tacit bond between an organization and its work force. Of course the other big benefit to the company is the low employee turnover. However, as the work force ages, this begins to work as a negative for the company. Long-term employees tend to receive more compensation than new, younger work-ers—even for the same amount of work. Mature workers are perceived as less innovative, and besides, their benefits (health, for example) are more expensive.

So how does a company change the culture of long-term employee/company loyalty without telling the workers? Well, the best time to introduce such a major shift in employer/employee relationships is dur-ing times of financial stress. For example, when an outside CEO is brought in to lead the company, he can list his own beliefs about what makes a modern and competitive company. Everybody will immediately begin quoting their new leader in this regard without bothering to understand what they lost. This they do in an effort to belong to the new regime. The original corporate policy statements may not even appear in the top ten tenets now officially recognized as gospel. One of the new publicized beliefs may be that the customer comes first. Well, in fact, the customer always did come first when it came to company policy. Does the hidden meaning behind such a phrase mean that the employee now comes fifth or sixth or even last?

Mature corporations found it advantageous to foster the notion that their employees could take personal problems to any management level in the corporation. This policy was sometimes referred to as the *open door policy*. In the past, even if workers never used this avenue to resolve an issue, they always knew they could count on management to listen to their gripes. However, to distance itself from dealing with such old-fash-ioned notions, today's corporate management delegates employee gripes to underlings such as the Human Resources Department or even appoints groups of individuals to deal with such issues. These subordinates have little power and are meant to assuage people's feelings rather than solve any problem. This fact quickly becomes known to the workers, but upper management feels good because less people are using the open door poli-cy than in past years. So the executives believe that the new policies are working beyond all expectations. What they miss is that the employees are only too quick to recognize what is happening, and resentment increases to such an extent that it adversely affects productivity and the willingness to work overtime.

Likewise, valued beliefs and policies that constituted the old corporate culture are increasingly dismantled. For example, the annual event that recognizes employees of twenty-five or more years of service suddenly disappears. Next, the quality (for example, the brand of watch gift) of the event that recognizes employees as they reach their twenty-fifth year of service is severely compromised. The message given to employees (both young and old) is that the company no longer values older workers.

How should you react to these signals? Simply put, you should look out for yourself and be willing to change companies whenever the opportunity presents itself. When dealing with your employer, treat the company merely as a vehicle to gain experience, because the company treats individuals as commodities that can be bought, forgotten, and discarded. Loyalty has been devalued.

Some Company Personality Types

~ of ~

Lords and Lackeys on Parade

As an employee in a large corporation, the variety of personalities you encounter in an everyday work environment is influenced by any number of variables. As the form of work changes, so does the disposition of the work force.

A look at a labor-intensive industry reveals that those jobs attract people who don't waste time talking about things. Those positions require individuals whose worth is determined by actions, not words. In this type of field it is easy to determine who is a productive worker and who is not. The measurement of physical effort is not difficult.

Personality traits in this labor-intensive field of endeavor include:

- ⤙ A direct manner of speaking so that there is little doubt as to what is intended
- ⤙ Taking responsibility to do what one says he or she can do
- ⤙ Less reliance on excuses when a job takes longer than expected

Now, in corporate America there is an awful lot of verbalization. So one's skill in the use of words becomes important. This facet allows a great deal of leeway in how one's assignments are performed. The correct use of vocabulary can place the burden of performing real or difficult work on one's peers while saving the task of reviewing or monitoring others' activities for the clever wordsmith artist or practitioner. This leaves you free to pursue other things. Because physical output is not generally required in the corporate world (thus making work measurement difficult), there is a lot of room for the development of personalities aimed at the appearance of doing work and having some fun besides. Pitches given, meetings attended, trips taken, and so on all affect the development of your corporate behavior.

Some of the most interesting personalities that occur in corporations include those in the following sections. Just pointing out these character types comforts naive employees by assuring them that others besides themselves actually experience such individuals.

The Ultimate Pitchman

This individual possesses a talent for giving presentations that is highly prized in large corporations. He skillfully employs all the latest techniques available in pitching subjects about which he may know very little. Does this bother him? No, he is enamored with his own ability to leave even the toughest of audiences with the impression that he is a technical wizard on almost every subject. Colored foils, multiple projection screens, and even background sound embellish his presentations to the masses. Even an inadvertent blank foil that appears in a pitch will not deter the ultimate pitchman. He merely treats a blank foil as part of his pitch and begins to illustrate (with a marker of some sort) some obscure point on the foil, all the while seeming completely at ease. He becomes so adept at *the art of the pitch* that he can present anyone's foils as if they were his own. Of course he does this without the benefit of any dialog with the original author. His services are in such high demand that he travels to distant outposts of the company to flash his message. His reputation continues to grow.

Now the real payoff in this scenario is his exposure to the corporate big boys—for this is how most of the executives attained their present positions (by always being able to deliver a good pitch). The executives tag him as a fast tracker able to joust with the best the company has to offer. Soon he is promoted to a corporate job. His opinion is sought on almost every subject because of his fame. Later in his corporate life, it is the ultimate pitchman who will become aware of another successful presenter and select him for corporate duty. So you can see that the cycle perpetuates itself. Pretty soon the corporate ranks are filled with pitchmen who never had to produce anything, and when a real crisis comes around, the big boys do what they do best. They give elaborate presentations to each other about the problem without ever taking any action.

So, the main objective of a good pitchman is to make a favorable impression no matter what. Never mind that it may distort the truth or alter the facts. No one seems to mind while under the spell of the ultimate pitchman.

The Technical Wizard

Often company managers let a *dominant technical personality* dictate company direction because either they don't have the talent to do it themselves or because a failed venture is career limiting. A pleasant side effect for management is that there is now a built-in fall guy if that direction fails. What often happens in reality is that the technical wizard becomes highly egocentric, possessing delusions of grandeur in her newly acquired position of power and title, and becomes unwilling to tolerate opposing opinions. This attitude quickly becomes known to the company's community of workers, and unwilling to endure the verbal abuse that accompanies such a leader, the workers isolate themselves from this abrasive personality. The result is that the organization ironically loses the creative abilities of numerous individuals—abilities for which the company hired them in the first place.

The *technical guru technique* may work in some situations, but in worst-case scenarios a *misguided direction* can go on for years, and ironically almost everybody knows it. Under a technical wizard's direction, people expressing a dissenting opinion are dismissed as non-team players resistant to change and even as incompetent laggards unwilling to learn the new technology. Just because an approach is new doesn't make it right. Remember the extrapolated adage "New technology can apply to all the situations some of the time or to some situations all of the time but never to all situations all of the time."

When a wizard is in charge, buzzword rebuttals supporting her viewpoint come into vogue, especially in large meetings where crowd intimidation plays an important role. She often quotes obscure testimonials that give credibility to her position. In this situation some sane individuals begin to doubt themselves. However, it is best to remember that when in doubt, *invoke logic.* It works every time. Soon, workers begin to see that the project is headed for a fall. However, some sycophants hoping to gain favor with the descending guru leap to her defense in the hopes that they can secure one last promotion or raise before her demise.

Soon, higher-level management realizes that a technical revolt is brewing within the company. At this point, the people in power, unwilling to admit that they made a mistake, promote the technical wizard to a position of total ineffectiveness. A title such as international/worldwide director of long-range strategic liaisons hides the fact that this person now has nothing to do. She is not invited to meetings, her office is downgraded, and perks (such as a private conference room) are taken away. She begins to count the days when she can leave, either through retirement or by obtaining a position with another unsuspecting employer.

Unfortunately, both the company and its workers lose in the long run because of opportunities that were pushed aside in favor of the wizard's pet projects. The blame rests solely on a management team too weak to comprehend what was happening.

The Psychotic Requirements Employee

An individual who determines what customers are willing to pay money for generally limits his information-gathering acquaintances to people who feel comfortable in the world of abstractness rather than reality. Rarely does he communicate with the worker establishment responsible for producing the actual product the customer wants. Soon, the psychotic requirements employee develops a working network that takes him to such exotic places as Europe and Asia. He convinces his manager that only by a *face-to-face* meeting with his peers can he accomplish his activities. His absence from the normal work location becomes routine, and the side effects of the travel soon take on an importance that exceeds the reason for traveling in the first place. Free first-class travel upgrades, free airplane trips, upgraded hotel accommodations, and new car rentals all begin to dominate his reason for travel. Meetings in warm climates have a predilection for occurring in the winter months. Ironically, high-level management relies on the psychotic requirements employee for strategic input about what the company should be producing. More high-level meetings are scheduled that contain an air of sincerity and urgency. The illusion of progress is enhanced by the amount of travel, meeting frequency, long hours, and elaborate pitches.

Meanwhile, back at the work location, individuals with the actual responsibility to produce something become nervous because of the absence of meaningful product requirements and begin to construct something that they believe satisfies customer needs. The worldwide meeting circus continues throughout the product development phase. Seldom does the psychotic requirements employee bother to see what is actually being developed. Only when the product is delivered, do meaningful customer requirements surface. All too often a mismatch has occurred. What occurs now is the task of *retrofit*, a euphemism that really means the customer thinks the product is a disaster and a redo is required.

The Fast Tracker

You can always tell the fast trackers from the regular, hard-working employees. They are identified early in their careers as movers and shakers. They seem to get the promotions and recognition even though they may not deserve them. Some of their attributes are as follows:

- ✎ Fast trackers are boundless handshakers at any formal or informal gathering of people. You can spot them because of this seemingly endless energy. This characteristic identifies them as outgoing, as people-oriented, and as individuals of broad interests. Never mind that they may forget who you are ten seconds after they pump your hand while flashing you a perfect smile.

- ✎ Fast trackers remain continually optimistic even in the face of impending disasters. This identifies them as loyal company men and women who always support the management in power. They seem to know that even if the present managers get removed, their recommendations go a long way in establishing the fast trackers' stature with the new management team.

- ✎ Fast trackers discuss topics outside of their normal work responsibilities even though they have no expertise in these other areas. Lacking knowledge never holds back any fast tracker. They make it a point to latch onto the latest buzz words and politically correct positions. This draws some respect from their fellow workers. However, more importantly, their immediate superiors who used this same technique are highly impressed. No subject is out of bounds. From marketing strategy to financial prospects to religious beliefs, their knowledge seems boundless to the unsuspecting.

- ✎ Fast trackers give the impression of working a great number of hours. They can easily accomplish this by arriving late undetected and then working a normal eight-hour workday. The conveyed perception is that fast trackers work overtime every evening. Aren't they hard workers?

- ✎ Fast trackers make sure they participate at important corporate gatherings, which are assigned with tasks of enormous importance. Never mind that they contribute nothing at the actual meetings that transpire. Back at the ranch, they verbalize the results to all who will listen as if the findings were their own. Notice that I used the word *verbalize* for fast trackers, because, as a group, they almost never write anything down for fear of making a mistake that can be traced back to them. Fast trackers are by nature fast talkers and can verbalize their way out of anything.

However, the most important attribute of a fast tracker is to emulate his or her boss. This is because, as you will find over and over again, managers tend to promote individuals who most mirror themselves. For example, when a woman gets promoted to an executive position, suddenly her area of responsibility becomes populated with a feminine cast. Similarly, people with marketing backgrounds surround themselves with people possessing the valuable commodity of *field experience*, even though people with technical skills in engineering and finance may actually be required.

The New Secretary

In today's office, the secretarial function is not performed by people called secretaries. Instead, those individuals are elevated to such obscure titles as administrative assistant or some kind of specialist. This sometimes causes them to acquire an air of professionalism that can interfere with their secretarial functions. For example, they may limit their duties to benefit only the person responsible for evaluating their performance. Thus, anyone who is not a manager soon discovers that he or she does not have access to secretarial services.

The corporate accountants have discovered that the plethora of personal computers make it possible for individual workers to do a lot of their own secretarial work, mostly at their own desks. Typing memos, making airline reservations, making copies, sending faxes, ordering office supplies, and so on have become the responsibility of each individual worker. Thus, you can witness highly paid professionals making copies at the copy machine and even fixing a paper jam. This problem compounds inefficiency because, often, trying to fix a machine when one knows nothing about it causes even more problems (like what will happen if someone pours black powder toner into the wrong receptacle).

But the accountants can accurately claim a cost savings in secretarial salaries. Here again they are missing the big picture. Consequently, the number of workers multiplies because of the inefficiencies now built into the workplace, and professionals—be they engineers, marketers, programmers, or analysts—continuously struggle with their secretarial duties while ignoring the jobs they are paid to do. Ironic but true.

Company Wannabes

To succeed in a corporate environment, the most direct route is to emulate those who are perceived to have made it. This tactic appears so ridiculous to rational employees that they think the copied individuals will sneer at such maneuvers. But copied individuals are either super-flattered, unaware of such happenings, or too occupied in their own careers to notice. This behavior perpetuates itself so that all the perceived movers and shakers in the company look and act alike.

Diversity is better than unquestioned imitation, but unfortunately conformity is the name of the game at large companies. If meetings are the mainstay of a successful individual's work habits, then meetings become the accepted way to function at work. If travel appears necessary to effectively perform one's duties, then get ready to join the gold and platinum frequent flier clubs. If gutter English is spoken in everyday discussions, then be prepared to limit your vocabulary to monosyllabic words that stun the uninitiated. If suspenders, cigars, dark suits, hard liquor, wing tips, and a protruding gut are the physical traits of the successful, then be prepared to gain weight, buy a new wardrobe, and become a health risk all for the sake of being thought a comer. A wannabe may assume a combination of all the traits of those thought of as successful.

Believe it—this activity assists one's career simply because of the perception it gives those in positions of power. If you think that just doing your job well is all you need to move up, be prepared to do that same job well over and over again for a number of years. People receive rewards based on what others perceive they have accomplished rather than what they actually do. Remember that in a large corporation, you can hide from doing any real work for years and thus have time to develop as a certified wannabe. Besides, it's more fun to play games than it is to produce something. Remember, if you never do anything, you can never make a mistake. Being thought of as mistake-free is a highly sought trait of the successful and powerful. People who never seem to make mistakes take every precaution so that if something they are remotely involved with fails, they can pull out memos written for this very purpose or cite conversations with other persons that place responsibility on others less astute at the game-playing activities.

Wannabes often quote the opinions and actions of successful people so as to convey the impression that they somehow contributed to those activities. Success by association works for many an ambitious employee, but to the thinking person it comes off as an empty means to an end.

The Corporate Gadfly

Some people just have a knack for irritating and annoying their fellow employees. It works better if these corporate gadflies also don't need their current jobs or any job for that matter. Owning a large block of stock in the company because of inherited wealth seems to help a lot. Such individuals are not afraid to say anything to anybody—even the corporate chairman. Although all employees must try to satisfy the needs of their their manager, this individual's manager cannot control the actions of the gadfly. Company rules for dress, travel, work schedules, and so on are for other employees less fortunate than the corporate gadfly. A distinct personality emerges as his reputation grows. He jumps from project to project, crisis to crisis, continent to continent with little accountability for his actions. It seems as if the major contribution of the corporate gadfly is to "stir up the pot."

However, real value can be realized from the behavior of such an individual. Usually his time is occupied by participating in task forces (a term borrowed from the military to emphasize urgency and importance). Such gatherings are supposed to solve problems of a particularly important nature. Now, it seems that task forces suffering through the participation of the corporate gadfly have a way of giving birth to thoughts, solutions, methods, and so on that were formerly dismissed for one reason or another. Why is it that most task forces are a waste of time, while gadfly-attended task forces occasionally produce something? It is because of some interesting phenomena. For example:

- The corporate gadfly has access to everyone in the company and isn't held back by the fear of losing his job in the face of championing an unpopular position. Therefore, the results of such a gathering cannot be easily ignored.
- Management makes sure its position is well represented and usually sends its best people to such meetings. This tactic serves the additional purpose of isolating management from the unpleasant occurrences of actual participation. Hence, ideas that were formerly repressed are warmly received by the corporate gadfly who relishes the thought of being unconventional.

Now, the corporate gadfly is not very popular with individuals who have opposing convictions about particular subjects. Tolerance is not one of the characteristics of a person used to having a free reign in the company. His antagonists become acutely aware that they are operating at a disadvantage and survive by distancing themselves from such an individual. However, they know that eventually he will make a fatal mistake. Over time the corporate irritant's methods (verbal abuse, intimidation, insults, and so on) wear thin with the company fat cats, so his tenure in this unofficial position begins to erode. Opponents rally when it becomes apparent that the gadfly is in trouble because he never bothered to cultivate a network of powerful allies who could help in a crisis. His ego fostered the notion that he needed no one and could do it all. "No man is an island" was never more valid than in a large corporation.

Marketing Fat Cats

Ever wonder why people with the most developed verbal skills end up in marketing? It is because they have learned that it is better to talk about something than to actually do it. That way, you can never make a mistake, and you get to criticize those who do. You also get to look at things from a more global perspective because details are for those who have specific duties. You become better educated by attending meetings to fill up the workday. Your allies in the company also have nothing tangible to do, so you become advocates of each other's contributions. Marketing fat cats often flatter their marketing peers, using phrases such as "John does an outstanding job," because it is accepted practice for them to lavish praise on others, hoping that John and other peers will say the same thing about them. Meanwhile non-marketing types are tied down to actually producing something, so they really don't have time to expose or interfere with a marketing person's activities.

Ironically, marketers see themselves as the movers and shakers in the company, for isn't it them who actually sell the company's products to its customers? Not so in a lot of cases, because:

- A company's products sell themselves if the company has the only game in town.
- Customers will order any new product produced by a leading-edge technical company to demonstrate to their competitors just how advanced they are.

⥅ Verbal people like being part of a team, so they become part of a marketing effort responsible for large accounts. This makes a perfect hiding place for people who are just along for the ride.

⥅ The difference between salesmen and order takers becomes a blur in big companies.

If any trips to coveted company locations are necessary for other functions in the corporation, you can be sure that the boys in marketing will wangle a way to travel there also. This is especially true if the location is Europe or Asia. Actually, it's not so bad to be accompanied by a marketing person when you're a legitimate participant on such a trip because you can be sure that the hotel accommodations, restaurants, rental car, and plane bookings will all be first class. So let marketing make all the reservations. They don't know how to travel any other way when the company is paying.

You can recognize marketing work areas by the number and variety of trinkets that decorate their offices. Each trinket represents some supposed accomplishment in their careers. Banners, paperweights, writing instruments, coffee cups, letter openers, plaques, and so on are all trophies to people attracted to this way of making a living. They also find it necessary to distinguish themselves from others in the company by other visible things, such as their type of dress, which schools they send their children to, house location, outside activities, and so on—all outward signs of success. Suits are their normal attire for lunching, attending a meeting, or just going to the restroom. They need to stand out in a crowd, and they view any outward sign toward this end as perfectly legitimate. To a marketer, it's the perception that counts.

In addition, marketing people promoted from field positions to jobs closer to headquarters find it advantageous to relive the action experienced in the trenches with their cohorts. This functions as a shared bond with co-workers in the same field and furthers their acceptance into the good-old-boy network. How does this differ from employees in other fields of endeavor? The degree of exaggerated experiences, frequency of discussion topic, one-upsmanship, and so on are all more predominant in a marketer's memory.

The Employee Who Must Verbalize

Certain individuals can't seem to get started on anything at work until they talk it over with others. A Type 1 verbal employee does this because he doesn't possess the knowledge, discipline, or work habits to initiate something. A Type 2 verbal employee possesses so much knowledge about the subject that he needs to talk just so he can eliminate extraneous information to focus his line of thinking toward the problem at hand.

The employee who must verbalize sometimes engages in conversation without bothering to hear the other communicator. It seems as long as he is talking, he is satisfied with the progress he is making. Any pictorials that he may draw to emphasize a point only possess meaning to their originator. Some drawings appear like something out of the museum of modern art. Needless to say, this type of employee irritates others because he barges into their offices just so he can talk.

The Information-Hiding Employee

Some employees collect information so that they appear to be the center of knowledge in their departments. This works to the individual's advantage because she always appears well-informed even though her everyday employee duties may suffer. She may even act as a spokesperson for the department because she seems to possess knowledge her peers lack.

The extreme of this type of worker is the employee who collects information but doesn't tell others of its existence. In effect, she hides it from her fellow employees. The information-hiding employee's advantage here is that as long as others are not aware of some particular subject, they can't participate in discussions that broaden their knowledge base. Thus, they appear uninformed and become less valued. This technique guarantees that only the information hider has access to data outside the normal work expectation and ensures her place in management's eye as the best-informed person in the department. Perhaps the information-hiding employee will even be put on the fast track because of her seemingly boundless information base.

The Quiet Employee

Employees who do whatever is asked of them can unknowingly cause misperceptions about their contributions to the company. This is especially true if the employee has a quiet personality in the workplace. If such an employee does everything asked of him, on time and with superior quality, others (especially his manager) begin to think that his performance is only good because he has been given easy assignments. Because of his quiet nature and excellent work habits, his dedication can backfire on him. Why? Because he never needs to redo assignments, attend high-profile crisis meetings, or work weekends to catch up. Therefore management doesn't even know who he is.

Consider the opposite type of personality, who complains constantly about the complexity of an assignment, works many hours of overtime, is always late completing assignments, and does work that has many flaws. Unless a manager is familiar with the actual work content and its demands (many managers do not even bother to understand what their employees actually do), she tends to think the complaining worker is doing a terrific job, considering all the obstacles he has told her about.

The Wordsmith Artist

The bigger the company, the more prolific and widespread the artists of verbosity are. These employees pretend to possess knowledge about every subject—buzzwords, products, strategy, tactics, schedules, real-estate values, the stock market, and so on. Just ask them. They gain popularity within the company because of the illusion they created that identifies them as members of the company's movers, shakers, and people in the know. They are smart enough, however, to avoid any discussion that may expose their surface knowledge. In any shoot-out with people who really understand these issues, they tend to be unavailable or to send a replacement because of "previous" commitments.

Because wordsmith artists get around in the company, they tend to surface whenever vacancies occur in slots requiring individuals adept at the dodge-and-weave game. (Briefly, dodging and weaving involves avoiding the shots your peers send your way because they are in trouble and want to drag others into their misfortune. Remember that sharing the blame is always better than taking a fall by yourself.)

The Esoteric Verbalist

Esoteric words, phrases, and acronyms spoken at opportune times give the illusion of tremendous knowledge, depth, and insight—especially when the audience is unaware of their existence. People even make these things up on the fly to impress their fellow workers.

Esoteric verbalists are especially effective when confronting a perceived adversary. In meetings, these catchy words/phrases dumbfound the opposition. The net result is that the esoteric verbalist successfully diverts your attention away from the actual meaning of the discussion because you are still unraveling the meaning of his latest buzzword. This technique works especially well on technically oriented listeners because it is their duty to be up on the latest happenings in their fields of endeavor. On the other hand, new verbiage does not faze most managers. They even incorporate the new vocabulary word into their word banks without fully comprehending its meaning. It seems as if it is an unwritten tenet that managers must always appear "in the know."

The Antagonist

Sometimes it seems that whatever you attempt to do, some people always say, "It's a bad idea," "It will never work," "You have legal problems," "Have you checked with marketing?" or "Why don't you do it this way?" They say this without hesitation and with the utmost confidence.

Now to the employee receiving such criticism, this can be a real downer. The effect of such a critical personality is to distract, undermine, impair, threaten, and otherwise confuse a perceived competitor. Without bothering to understand what you are saying, antagonists launch into a verbal assault that can attack your integrity, your understanding of the issues, your dress, your ethnic heritage, or other subjects outside the work environment (for example, even your selection of investments). Antagonists feel that no matter what you are involved with, they are better, and you are wrong.

Antagonists tend to be loud, domineering, in need of a stage, and resentful of anything not directly attributed to their activities. They subconsciously form alliances with others who have these same traits because they do not want to incur the wrath of such a person. On occasion, when such an encounter does occur, the ensuing confrontations can be quite ugly.

The best ways to survive an antagonist's assault is to ignore him or her whenever the discussion occurs one-on-one, and to resort to calm, forceful, informed rebuttal in the presence of an audience. You need to deal immediately with any negativism that was expressed in the presence of others, because if you say nothing, others will give credibility to the antagonist. Above all, never lose your cool, for this is a sign that you have run out of logical reasoning.

The Agreeable Worker

Ever wonder why individuals who are non-controversial at work always seem to move up the promotion ladder faster than those who rely on advancement based on merit? It's simple: Those doling out the perks see congenial employees as team players who possess "the right attitude." Now, the word *attitude* has been used to disguise a plethora of ailments associated with those who have different outlooks on various subjects than management does. The phrase "Joe Employee simply doesn't have the right attitude" can cause your career demise quicker than if you contracted leprosy.

Cooperative employees are easy to manage mainly because of their docile attitude. It is always easy to win a discussion with an agreeable person because she wants to agree with you even before the confrontation begins. Besides, she reasons, it is always better to agree with a supposed authority even though he may be in error. To an agreeable employee, the expression "to compromise is to win" is acceptable. Conversely, activists may be looked upon as impeding progress even though they may be alerting others about the folly of a department's endeavor.

The Rumormonger

The unsuspecting individual is led to believe that company bulletin boards (both physical and electronic) serve the purpose of keeping everyone informed about current events. Now, you as an employee must recognize that only the occurrences and viewpoints that the company wants you to digest are ever prominently displayed. So the official company information barrage becomes a lucrative avenue that attempts to steer the thought perspectives of its employees. Subjects unpopular with employees usually appear in multi-page newsletter articles (hoping no one bothers to read them) or announcements that are only posted for a day or afternoon (hoping no one sees them)—or they are couched in obfuscation (information that is clouded). Enter the company rumormonger.

A rumormonger has various ways of obtaining the information he communicates to his peers. Origins of company gossip can be obtained from sources such as (1) conversations at the coffee machine, (2) e-mail to/from his comrades at other geographical locations, (3) subtle signals pieced together to arrive at a conclusion worthy of the status of a rumor, (4) something told to him in confidence by his manager, (5) accidental access to privileged data (for example, an original sheet of paper left in the copy machine), and (6) multiple related rumors giving birth to a new rumor.

Official confirmation doesn't seem to matter as long as a good proportion of his rumors proves to be true. The time lapse for information verification can be long, and it becomes important to a rumormonger that predictions of the future are attributed to him first. A sort of informal competition exists among individuals wanting to be the "official rumor-monger." Fellow workers and even managers seek these people out to feel "in the know."

The Disgruntled Employee

If an employee is not laboring at the best job attainable, she should be looking for another position. It's that simple. Yet most individuals criticize their present employers for their unfulfilled expectations. It's not disloyal to aspire to greater things. It is, however, a sign of immaturity to whimper as a child. Now, circumstances may inhibit or even prevent this employee from taking immediate action to correct this perceived shortcoming. Nevertheless, a future opportunity will probably surface that theoretically matches her perceived skills and worth. What transpires in the meantime? Unfortunately, most workers usually advertise their predicaments by voicing disparaging remarks about their current employers. They may attack their immediate manager's competence, the company's benefit plan, the salary plan, promotional opportunities, or whatever, but none of this acerbic verbiage can change the employee's present situation. Only she can effect change, but she does not easily recognize this solution. Instead, she becomes frustrated. The complaints become chronic, and the deserved reputation as a distressed trooper becomes associated with unhappy Jill Employee. (By the way, a disgruntled employee can appear at any level in the corporate job classification system.)

The disparaging atmosphere festers and eventually contaminates the thinking of fellow workers. It's easy to be drawn into the growing circle of discontent. Discussions dwelling on the negatives seem to occupy a large part of the working day. Others may become unhappy with their individual situations without understanding exactly why. Not only can the work situation become unpleasant, but life outside work can be similarly affected.

However, the experienced employee has witnessed such occurrences of discontent before. He believes it is best to distance himself from this pessimistic activity, and one of the best techniques to avoid such entanglements is to become more involved in everyday work activities. Many seasoned workers have a way of manipulating their assignments to attain a degree of satisfaction that is not fully understood by those who administer or those who whine. He has learned to find solutions on his own rather than look for someone else to solve these kinds of problems. His example can influence other malcontents to return to the ranks of the gainfully employed. After all, the company pays its workers to produce something—anything.

Eventually, the unhappy employee gets another position, which she believes exploits her talents better than the previous job. She believes the new position provides better career opportunities. Only time will reveal whether this is, in fact, true.

Conclusion

Employees of a large corporation have a diversity of backgrounds and duties that influence and/or determine how they interact with their fellow workers. By being aware of such personality diversities and subtle games people play, you will be better able to cope with such annoyances and focus on the job at hand.

Procedures in Large Companies

~ or ~

Who Needs Reasons When We Have Policies?

Within any large corporation, procedures exist to ensure that there is some order to the everyday business operation. What follows is a look at some of these procedures and the absolute absurdity of how some of them are actually practiced.

The Specious Product Commitment Procedure

Whenever commitments are made to introduce a new product into the marketplace, the promises usually start at the top. A high-ranking corporate executive promises an important customer that her needs will be met with the new whizbang gizmo the company is presently working on. In reality, no one in product development has the faintest notion that the department is supposed to be working on this gizmo. So, a rash of activity unfolds as lower-ranking managers become aware of their plight. These managers begin to avidly push for this new product, often quoting that Company X wants it, the marketplace demands it, and after all, "We work for a world-class company." To curry favor with their superiors, lower-level management makes commitments based on the product delivery date that higher-ranking executives have set. Everybody says it will be difficult to meet the schedule dictated by the high-ranking executives.

Meanwhile, the actual workers are busy trying to meet prior product commitments made several years ago. (Even unsuspecting college students currently engaged in academic achievement will probably work on this as-yet-undefined product.) Now it comes time for the workers who will actually produce the product to be told of the commitment. "No way," "ridiculous," "absurd," and other expletives can be heard in the hallways. Finally, after much arm-twisting, the workers say they will try to meet the schedule. As the product finds its way through the development cycle, what the customer requested only vaguely resembles what she will get.

The Performance Review

Periodically, employees must endure evaluations by their managers, even though some managers haven't the faintest idea what their employees do. How can a manager inject some relevance into his review of an employee? He simply asks others what they think of the employee's work. So once again, the illusion you project determines how this process turns out. You can't rely on just doing your job. You need to publicize to others how good you really are. One irony is that if you perform your job without any perceived crisis, you will probably not be held in high regard. The adage "the squeaky wheel gets the grease" was never more true than in corporate life.

To facilitate this performance review, the Human Resources Department provides standard forms. Because the manager completes this form before your meeting, you may be caught cold as to how to respond to uncomplimentary comments. You may be asked to sign the form even though you may disagree with its content. You also may be told that even though you sign it, it does not mean you agree with it. Experience shows that it is better not to sign such a contentious review because people in the chain of command only look to see if your evaluation was completed. They don't care about individual ratings because there are simply too many. But an unsigned review is interpreted as a manager delinquent in performing a duty (paperwork) in which he is expected to excel.

Management attempts to give the impression that it distributes money allocated for raises based on the rating you receive in the performance evaluation. This is done to support the illusion that all pay raises are based on merit and is meant to inspire employees to work even harder. In reality, most raises are given to keep up with the cost of living, to counteract a competitor's lucrative offer to join another company, to bring an employee's compensation up to the level received by others doing the same work (she may have been treated unfairly by preceding management), or to distribute the company's plentiful profits to give the perception of paternal benevolence.

In times of economic distress, companies have come up with the following excuses for granting no raises:

- ✎ "You are at the top of the grid for your performance and job level, so raises will be less frequent and smaller."
- ✎ "Part of your pay will be based on how well the company is doing, and you can receive up to X percent (for example, ten) of your compensation this way." Of course this option is never offered when economic times are good. So guess what: The variable pay percentage never materializes for years on end when profits are disappointing.
- ✎ "The company's new ranking method indicates that you are overpaid for what you do compared with what others receive for the same type of work.
- ✎ "This company has traditionally paid a ten percent premium to its workers, and we are just aligning salaries with industry standards."

The Infamous Opinion Survey

At last, the means to express employee viewpoints regarding the company's management, working conditions, salaries, and so on has been freely bestowed upon the common worker. It is called the opinion survey, and it contains questions that you are led to believe can soothe your conscience by allowing you to blow off steam.

Now, the first thing people should notice is that the questions are provided by the management. So employees' thoughts are guided to particular areas where management wants them, rather than areas that have been gnawing at workers for some time. Most of the time, the company repeatedly urges you to be frank because anonymity is assured. However, you soon may learn that the questionnaire contains questions and statements like (1) Are you male or female? (2) How long have you been employed by the company? (3) Identify your middle management, and (4) Select your job description.

Now, *anyone* can identify who responded to each question. To make it easier, the company sometimes puts the questionnaire on-line and so, by accessing it electronically, you can be easily identified without the possibility of human error. No guesswork will be involved.

The day of the survey brings great joy to the employees because they believe that finally they can tell management what they *really* think of their jobs. The people in control may even tell you that there will be a review of the results with your department manager. You feel good. But when the day of the review arrives, the presented results may be watered down. First, you may learn that if you didn't respond in the extreme positive or negative, say on a scale of 1 to 5 (where 1 is super and 5 is the pits), then your response was considered neutral. Next, your department will be compared with other departments, and even though your department's results were extremely poor, the summary may show that your department is better than most. Now that's the way to make something positive out of extreme negativism.

Next comes management's action plan. This misnomer gives you hope that management will do something about survey areas that were particularly negative. But often, having a plan doesn't mean anything will happen. The word *plan* is often used in delicate situations to assure the masses that everything will be all right. For example, a product plan may not reflect reality, but you will still hear over and over again that, *according to the plan, the product is on schedule, within cost, and meeting the quality objectives.* Reality is not always publicized to the workers, let alone top management. After all, the middle managers who are responsible for the product depend on their superiors for continued financial funding and, most important, their next promotion. So bad news is routinely hidden. You would think top managers would know this game because many of them played it in the early days of their careers. But no, everyone continues working, hoping everything will work out in the end. Guess what! The workers know the truth because every day brings them face-to-face with the real world. They begin to disregard what management tells them because they perceive that this communication is freely sprinkled with euphemisms.

Finally, even though you may have been told that a department meeting would be scheduled to reveal the survey's results, sometimes the results of an opinion survey are so universally poor that the meeting never materializes. Then the yearly survey may be delayed for several years. Does management think the workers are not sharp enough to catch on to what is happening?

The Exit Procedure

At the end of your career in the company, watch out for the exit procedure. First of all, the manager may schedule the exit interview for you after the end of the last normal workday to squeeze the most work out of you before you go. This even happens to employees who have worked thousands of unpaid overtime hours for the company, where they have been employed for more than thirty years. Why should you even pay attention to him? For one reason, he has your final paycheck with accrued vacation time. For another, he has to mark a box on the exit checklist to indicate whether you are eligible for re-hire, should you in the future want to work for this same company. You then must sign a legal-sounding statement, saying you will not use intellectual information gained during your employment at the company to benefit a competitor. But your experience is what other companies are willing to pay for, so whether this is enforceable or not is debatable. Still, the signed statement somehow makes people feel that their skills belong to the company they are leaving.

Sometimes you may receive some sort of severance allowance because of a layoff or because of some other reason, such as "It is to the company's and employee's advantage to terminate your employment." Beware! To protect themselves against repercussions by employees who may subsequently realize injustice has been done, companies often require you to sign a statement that makes you responsible for their legal costs in case you decide to seek justice in the country's court system. Pretty slick? You bet. No signature, no severance pay.

Interestingly enough, you are almost always guaranteed some sort of severance pay if you are judged an undesirable worker. In other words, if you are a bad employee you will receive money to leave, whereas if you are a good employee and leave because of some distress, you probably won't receive any monetary compensation. At first glance this looks OK. From the company's viewpoint, one termination is involuntary and the other voluntary, and people who elect to leave are not eligible for severance pay. But companies won't publicize that the definitions of voluntary and involuntary employment termination are left up to their own interpretation. Why is this done? Simply put, it saves the company money.

How a company handles an employee's departure is an indication of the company's confidence in itself, as well as its true regard for the people aspects of employment. In periods of growth, good management, and economic well-being, the employee usually receives a celebration, together with a gift. Management may even sponsor this event in the hopes of conveying the perception that the company is a benevolent employer to the end. Actually, it benefits management to terminate an individual's employment on good terms because he will always speak highly of his former employer, especially to his co-workers at the new company.

Contrast this type of departure with one that occurs when management is myopic, lacking in people skills, or under pressure to squeeze employees for productivity—or when management just doesn't care. In these instances, exiting employees sometimes are told they have fifteen minutes to clear their desks before they are escorted out the door by a security officer. No mention is usually made of Joe Employee's reason for leaving—or even that Joe left. The effect of this type of departure is to convey a feeling of insecurity, insensitivity, and callous management. Of course the departing employee will always feel resentful when he discusses his former employer.

Next, let's take a look at the voluntarily departing worker who is respected by her peers and was pushed by management into the fast lane. The company cannot simply shuffle her out the door, because she was one of the anointed fast trackers. Yet management is understandably upset that Jill Employee has found a better job. Too often, the company will subtly retaliate by making Jill work overtime until the very end, giving her the exit interview at the end of her last working day (on her own time), and delaying her final paycheck for about two weeks after she leaves.

"Standard" Procedures

Companies feel a sense of accomplishment when they adhere to procedures (for example, an International Standards Organization [ISO] decree) that others define. They even advertise their conformance to these methods, believing that it adds a degree of respectability or "stamp of approval" to their product/service output. Consumers are led to believe that goods and services that follow a standard procedure are better than those that do not.

Adhering to standard methods adds a degree of comfort because it removes responsibility from its practitioner. A standard may even be scoffed at, but it offers a safe road to job security. It's a substitute for having to think. Mental exercise requires effort and does not guarantee correct results. It's easy to respond whenever anyone questions the necessity or even validity of a process. Just answer, "It's standard procedure." This reply usually disarms and satisfies the person asking the question. Some employees even admit that they hide behind standard procedures.

In a large number of situations, the lack of standard procedures would cause individuals undue stress because of the uncertainty that would occur every day at the office. New employees experience this feeling until they learn the ropes. Standards are useful when they are applied to repetitive processes that require little judgment. Otherwise, they hinder the thinking process.

Conclusion

On the surface, corporations institute certain procedures to efficiently manage their large enterprises. In their implementation these processes can deviate from their objectives so that thinking employees become annoyed and frustrated. Come to appreciate the pitfalls and humor that such conventions provide.

Games People Play

~ of ~

How to Spot Houdini, Copperfield, and Other Masters of Illusion

Some employees look upon the activities that transpire in the workplace as contests that produce winners and losers. In many respects, that is exactly how the work environment should be viewed to maintain the correct perspective. For if you do not bother to learn the unwritten rules of the many games that are played, it could affect your sanity, as well as your career.

The Promotion Game

When it comes time to promote individuals within an organization, management can be severely restricted in its choice of promotees because of subconscious influences. For example, the promoters may yield to the whim of their immediate management (thereby enhancing their own upward mobility), satisfy an unmentioned government quota for gender and/or ethnic background, or favor candidates possessing similar backgrounds as themselves. Also, a particular individual may be promoted to a position where she can do no harm if it becomes clear that she can't do her current work assignments.

The practice of promoting because of background similarity is especially harmful. Take the case where a marketing background is the common experience. What happens is that marketing people soon dominate company positions that require skills such as engineering, finance, and so on. Often, these individuals are so busy living in the world of smiles and handshakes that they don't even realize they may be in deep trouble. They rely on catchy phrases (which work in a sales job), such as world class, customer driven, or industry leader. These words only increase the gap between management and the individuals who have the responsibility to produce something. Such managers often expect things to work out by themselves—without their leadership. Unfortunately, just having the title of manager—whatever your background—doesn't solve anything without action. Molding your dress, vocabulary, and behavior to emulate your boss can have an enormous effect on the importance management places on you. Smoking cigars, wearing cowboy boots, putting your feet on the conference table during a meeting, and so on can all help convey that you are just like the boss.

This technique works and sustains itself until it comes time to produce something. At this time the people promoted into positions of authority can't lead or produce because they are only skillful at acting out a part, as in a play or movie. These and other illogical occurrences can all happen while management is championing promotion based on merit.

The Planning Game

In companies of all sizes, there exists a need to plan both updates to existing products and future products to generate revenue in the upcoming years. In theory, planning encompasses obtaining cost estimates, customer requirements, competitive analyses, shipping schedules, and the like. This is an important function, but unfortunately not much *real* planning actually occurs.

Why is this true? First, little planning takes place because the planning team generally consists of people who unfortunately view their time in planning as a stepping stone to bigger things. Therefore, they spend most of their efforts lobbying for their next job at corporate.

Second, recognizing that the planning team needs individuals with analytical skills, management may sell product developers on the notion that planning is a growth path that will broaden their skills. In reality, planning attracts developers because it is viewed as an easier job than product development. Nebulous schedules, commitments, duties, loyal-tics, and so on all contribute to the attractiveness of such a job. Account-ability is often lost because the job itself requires frequent travel, endless meetings, and assignments that focus on the current hot buttons of company executives, who view planners as their private political buffer from competing administrators.

Perks also accompany the travel part of planning. Airlines award points that accrue toward free trips, as well as free upgrades to first-class seating. Hotels have seen the value of the frequent traveler and similarly award free stays. Because of the perception of importance conveyed by frequent travel to distant locations, planning people sometimes begin to believe that they are the movers and shakers of the company. When they do their jobs correctly, planners can contribute much to the company. Unfortunately, many planners do little real planning.

The Architecture Game

The architectural phase of a product's life should be considered the product's most important component. The people who compose the group that defines the product often are talented individuals who want to do the right thing. Unfortunately, business pressures, political differences, product standards, schedules, customer acceptance, and the like all contribute to trade-offs made during the architectural phase. For example, products that make it to market first, set standards that seem to last forever—even if the standard is recognized as inferior to other proposals addressing the same problem. Thus, instead of the best possible product, what is architected is most often a compromise.

Members of such an organization often come from product development groups, for members of these groups are most familiar with the inner workings of the existing products. They know the problems and are most valuable in architecting extensions to what they know and understand. However, the company often does not listen to their vision of the future because it has stereotyped these people as present-day technologists. It's too bad because, by ignoring them, the company loses a valuable insight.

Occasionally, people are hired directly from academia to work in this architectural group. Many of these people lack real experience but quickly master the game of management presentations. Their most valuable skill is the art of the presentation. In some respects, it is unfortunate they can verbalize so well: Practical experience may elude them for their entire careers if they work for a company that is enamored by (and that quickly promotes) people who talk a good game. These individuals may embellish a well-known concept so as to promote the proposal as both new and, most importantly, their own. On the other hand, new hires from academia placed in developmental positions may leave in disgust if they see a wordsmith's advancement while they toil nights and weekends trying to perfect a product.

But when one of these architects' visions is a complete disaster, management must sit up and take notice. Management doesn't usually want to openly criticize the disastrous choice because it would be an indictment of management's own judgment too. So failure may be softened with such euphemisms as "It was too far ahead of its time," "It's cheaper to extend the current products with proven technology," "We can't obsolete our present revenue-producing products," and "It was a terrific idea, but unfortunately development botched the implementation."

The most successful transfer of product responsibility from the architectural phase to the developmental phase occurs when architecture has done a selling job to get development to buy into the idea. Only if people believe in what they are doing will they perform at their best. Often products fail because no buy-in has transpired. The second best way to ensure a successful transfer is to transfer the architectural people who defined the product to the corresponding development group, to demonstrate their commitment to the idea. After all, don't they know the most about what development is supposed to build?

The Task Force Game

Task forces are bred out of a perceived business emergency that could not be contained within the normal corporate operating environment. Management is eager to show others that the problem is being addressed. So as long as management can assign bodies to the unexpected issues at hand, it usually feels it is doing its job. Sometimes management does not even feel it is important to assign the right people to the task force, because often the problem and the expected output of the assembled task force is never clearly stated. Experience has demonstrated that if a task force has a large number of participants for a lengthy period of time, then others will perceive this effort with high regard. Unfortunately, all too often the quality of the task force is inversely proportional to the number of its members. Time can be wasted just trying to figure out what the task force is being asked to address.

For participants, there is a plus side of being selected to serve on a task force. For one thing, important discussions usually occur in sunny climates during the winter months. In addition, visibility to upper management is usually guaranteed to task force participants. Now, representatives from various groups within the company may have different agendas. For example, it is not unusual for a task force member to be told by his superiors to make sure that any responsibility to solve the problem does not find its way into his area of management. Another hidden agenda may be to disrupt the task force to such an extent that its failure is assured. Why would someone do this deliberately? Simply put, the task force may be investigating a competing alternative that would detract from a particular management area of responsibility.

When the output of the task force becomes known before its conclusion, it is interesting to see how many people swing their support to the winning side. Sometimes people do not even find it necessary to know what the details of the outcome are—they just support the viewpoint of those personalities they know to be politically connected.

If it becomes known that a particular task force is about to reach a conclusion opposite of the conclusion desired by the company, the leadership of the group may be usurped by a high-ranking manager, who *guides* members of the group to the politically correct solution. Once the official position of the task force becomes known (right or wrong), that position often becomes quoted dogma for any doubting Thomas. It's as if the task force was a blessed event anointed by the powers in control. So rather than representing the opinions of an unbiased gathering of talented individuals, many task force solutions seem to have a way of favoring political correctness.

A Task Force Extravaganza

Every once in a while, opportunity presents itself in the form of a task force that is destined for ultimate prominence in the corporation. Such occurrences often happen because a high-level manager needs to accelerate her visibility in order attain a top executive position. Unfortunately, sometimes it doesn't even matter if there is a real need for the task force. Now, other ambitious executives may not fully cooperate in such an endeavor because their participation in an event of such magnitude would reduce their roles to simply supporting the ideas of a perceived rival. Let the games begin.

Such sanctioned gatherings usually spare no expense. The bigger, the better. It seems as if the more they cost, the more the desired notoriety is achieved in the corporation. It is not unusual to kick off the extravaganza with a sit-down meal (say, a country club breakfast) with all the participants in attendance. Now in a multi-location organization, the company's sites may include facilities on the East Coast, West Coast, and wherever. So travel is a big expense. It doesn't seem to matter that people fly across the continent for breakfast and then leave right after breakfast to return home.

In its implementation, the gala task force is usually sequestered in an off-site location. This adds to its importance and mystique. Such action is justified under the guise that no partakers should be bothered by the distractions of their regular jobs.

Weekly reviews are usually conducted to monitor the progress of the gala event. During these reviews, individuals leading various groups within the task force may be required to expose their findings to a roomful of barracuda inquisitors. Asking questions and requesting clarification can lend some degree of credibility to audience members bent on using the occasion to bolster their own career goals. They may figure that the more vocal they are, the more others (perhaps people in high-level management jobs) will notice their verbal skills. The game of dump-and-verify usually begins when a questioner makes a harsh critique concerning some point (about which he may only have the slightest hint of knowledge) made by the presenter. He then asks the presenter to verify that the critique he just made is, in fact, true. Pretty slick. Good charts help, but the art of wordsmithing pays bigger dividends. After several presentation experiences, the presenter's objective is to just get by the hostile reviewers.

How long will these important meetings go on? Six months can easily pass without much progress. Then executives may sense the time has come to terminate the gathering, so they declare its successful conclusion—even though there still may be much controversy and debate.

The Reorganization Game

Valid rationale does exist for organizations within corporations to undergo a reorganization. However, the real reasons are sometimes disguised by a management bent on remaining in power, gaining power, spreading the illusion of being progressive, and so on. The managers of a reorganization often come to rely on phrases such as: "to enhance our understanding," "to better focus," "to centralize the company's expertise," or even "to achieve synergism." Beware of these phrases because they are frequently employed to mask the real reasons behind the reorganization.

Do employees fall for this propaganda? Well, after the first three or four overhauls, they become skeptical and begin to look for any changes that occurred that do not relate to the official hypothesis. (Note that veteran workers also notice changes that *did not* occur.) One common deception is to define a manager's activities in a fashion so it appears that her duties have increased. For example, she could have a continuing management responsibility for a first-line department plus another manager who reports to her. It appears as if she has acquired the role of a second-line manager in addition to her original responsibility. In reality, both departments may function as before, but on an organization chart the alignment looks impressive to upper management.

A variation of this maneuver is to have additional departments report to a manager for "functional guidance." Now, *guidance* is a word that allows a lot of leeway in its interpretation. To guide someone, you do not actually have to get involved with producing anything.

A reorganization can also help remove a manager from power. Unfortunately, the dethroned manager need not be incompetent. Maybe her superiors just don't like her for a number of reasons. Such treatment usually is not open to appeal; this method can offer a discrete "out" for top executives, because it must not appear that they made a mistake in their choice to employ this person. Individuals who are experiencing this finesse are usually given nebulous (or even no) duties. So the phrases "being placed in a holding pattern" and "being put in the penalty box" are most appropriate. In large corporations, this state of employment can last for quite a long time. Sometimes it becomes a test of will power between the employee and the ousting management. In such a situation, several avenues are open to the employee. A few are listed below:

- ➷ She can resign. If this happens, the company saves in severance pay and the embarrassment of an actual firing.
- ➷ The deposed manager can explore other management opportunities within the company. It is important to have a network of friends in this instance.
- ➷ The manager can occupy her time with self-education so she can re-enter the ranks of the working-class employees.
- ➷ She can just wait out her time in the penalty box with the expectation that her talents will be recognized by subsequent management.

In addition, a reorganization can offer an excuse for management to get rid of employees under the illusion of efficiency. What happens to the displaced workers? Companies can use a variety of methods to promote their image as good corporate citizens. A favorite is to shift responsibility of the layoffs to an outside firm specializing in displaced people. This outside firm usually offers classes, counseling, and other pleasant-sounding services that attempt to assuage the impact of an actual layoff. They may tell you of great opportunities with fantastic incomes. In the end, however, you are told that *you*, the displaced employee, are responsible for finding your own job.

What happens to the employees who survive the cutback? First, you are probably expected to be grateful that you still have a job. Second, because the terminated employees must have been doing some work, your work load incorporates their duties. You may find yourself working nights and weekends just to keep up.

Beware of reorganization because it can also give companies an excuse to lower the performance ratings of employees. This can be especially true for senior workers who performed adequately in their prior assignments. For example, when a department consists entirely of newly reorganized, highly ranked employees, an unspoken HR quota system comes into play. This promotes the notion that employees in a department must follow the company guidelines that allot certain percentages of employees to performance categories, such as:

- ⇥ 10 percent should be ranked "superior."
- ⇥ 20 percent should be ranked "above average."
- ⇥ 40 percent should be rated "meets requirements."
- ⇥ 20 percent should be ranked "fails to meet requirements."
- ⇥ 10 percent should be rated as "eligible for dismissal."

Remember that occurrences of reorganization give the illusion that something grand has just occurred. Look deeper for other agendas.

The Workaholic Illusion Game

Individuals wishing to convey the impression that they are dedicated employees willing to sacrifice their private lives for the good of the company often put in eighty, ninety, or even one hundred hours per week. They usually perform this feat in a fashion such that everyone is aware that they are resorting to such Herculean efforts. Good press is always healthy for their perceived reputations (especially when it comes time for their performance reviews). What other co-workers may not know is that these workaholics are probably receiving overtime compensation and therefore may be deliberately wasting time on the job (for example, by playing cards). However, their work habits often still impress both their peers and their bosses. Stop to think, and you will realize that after fifty hours per week, your efficiency drops off enormously.

Exactly what can consume so much time? Workaholics often can make toll-free calls to friends using the company's watts line during off-hours.

They may also take care of their financial affairs with their stockbrokers during normal working hours—and then receive extra compensation for overtime hours (plus travel reimbursement and meal payments). They can even manage private businesses of their own from their desks, all while getting paid by the company.

The irony of this *modus operandi* is that such employees are often held up as models to others by a naive management. The workaholic's ruse has the undesirable effect of contributing to the subsequent low morale and productivity of other knowledgeable co-workers.

The Administrative Assistant Game

The purpose of the administrative assistant game is to give accelerated experience to people who excel at their jobs. These people are hence designated administrative assistants to serve alongside high-level mentors. This move is usually looked upon by its recipients as an opportunity to bypass the normal promotion ladder. This corporate venture becomes most popular to demonstrate to both sideline and worker-bee players the idea that good work merits recognition. Unfortunately, this perk is often reserved for people in management, so a technical worker never gets the benefit of working directly for a high-level mentor.

The negative of this administrative assistant policy is that the employee who has excelled at his job is snatched from the ranks of those making real contributions. Some administrative assistants never return to the class of the gainfully employed because their experience teaches them that real work involves risk, whereas in high-level management work, lower-level workers take risks, and those who work at the higher levels get to critique their work. Large corporations are full of people who criticize, but there always seems to be a shortage of people who "do."

The actual administrative assistant job may easily deteriorate into the job of a gofer. If this happens, you are probably doomed to the ranks of the also-rans. But if the role is played right, it can lead to a position of greatly increased money and power that lasts for your entire career. So make the best of this opportunity by developing a good rapport with your mentor. This rapport is best enhanced by emulating the work habits of your mentor. Especially noteworthy are transoceanic airline flights arriving in the morning at some foreign airport immediately followed by a fifteen-hour workday. Again, it's not important that you are dead-tired and can't possibly do an adequate job (whatever it may be). What is important is that your fellow workers marvel at your stamina, dedication, and appearance of being a real comer. You may develop a certain swagger that marks you as an "anointed one." Your vocabulary may immediately expand so you can adequately discuss more global subjects, such as inter-divisional development, European markets, international standards, currency differences (useful when corporate profits are low), and so on. Initiation into the ranks of the big corporate players almost always takes the form of immense amounts of time spent working—or at least giving the appearance of working. Others in the company will most likely be painfully aware of your status, and they will probably treat you with the respect that is due your mentor because they know you have the ear of a powerful manager.

After your "assistantship tour" is complete (about 1 to 1.5 years in duration), you will probably be given a high-level job, usually somewhere within the organization of your former mentor. How can you lose? Everyone in the organization knows of your special relationship with your mentor and acts accordingly. Former mentors evolve into godfathers over time.

The Godfather Game

In your quest for recognition, promotion, power, status, and so on, having someone who is looking out for your welfare is a most necessary ingredient for you to reach a high-level corporate job. Although merit does carry some weight for promotion at the lower levels in a corporation, positions associated with money and power are reserved for those with special status. Often, both parties (the one bestowing favoritism and the one receiving it) are unaware (in the beginning) that this special relationship even exists. Of course neither would ever admit it, for in the corporate game, preferential treatment is not supposed to exist. The in-word for this unspoken association is *godfather*. How might such a relationship develop? Here are but a few examples.

- ✦ Let's say your work directly contributed to making your future godfather look good in some recognizable crisis situation. This act forms a tacit alliance that your future godfather will always remember. Fortunately, godfathers usually restrict the number of such designated people to one or two. Higher numbers would dilute this special relationship.

- ✦ Let's say you are most adept at winning arguments. It doesn't matter whether you are right, wrong, or totally ignorant of the subject being discussed. What is critical is that you always appear to win. This is most important. Your future godfather would rather see you as an ally instead of an adversary. Therefore, he is able to somewhat control you because he appears to be looking out for your welfare.

↔ Let's say you and your future godfather possess some bond outside of work, such as the school you both attended or even the school you both did not attend. For example, some professional employees who did not attend college seem to form unspoken relationships with each other when this fact becomes known. Other commonalties include military service, similar value systems, hometowns, and an interest in sports. These types of bonds exist for most everyone. Ambitious individuals usually popularize these past experiences to gain some advantage over their competitors.

Whenever a godfather relationship develops, your fellow workers will probably be quick to spot this occurrence. It may not be immediate, but soon everyone will understand that this tacit association exists. People survive in this environment by speaking only positive things about both parties in the presence of one or the other, for each of these individuals usually thinks highly of the other. Unfortunately for the company, the negative side of such affiliations is that honest evaluation regarding anything negative associated with godfather participants usually becomes muffled.

Having a godfather is absolutely essential for you to achieve the higher ranks within the corporate hierarchy.

Management's Misuse of the Overtime Game

When management shifts the game of overtime into overdrive, the outcome is usually not what was intended by the notion of working extra hours. Some managers try to instill a sense of urgency into the lower-level ranks by resorting to the tactic of "making them sweat." Its manifestation is as follows. A high-level manager may reveal to her subordinates that she will work twenty hours extra each week until a perceived crisis is over. (Note that the subordinates are usually all exempt from receiving overtime pay.) Whether or not a real need for overtime exists, however, is often irrelevant because the purpose is to intimidate employees into working more hours for reasons of the manager's personal gain. For example, overtime can:

- ↪ Impress her competing peer-management structures with the amount of extra effort being put forth by her region of responsibility. Note that the organization makes regular departmental comparisons of the number of overtime hours being clocked by various areas. Although this may be a measure of productivity in a manufacturing effort, it can be most detrimental to people who earn their livings by making creative contributions to the company.
- ↪ Foster the notion of a crisis to maintain power. In such cases overtime can be mandated to impress upon everyone just how serious the emergency illusion is. Some rational workers may even object to this mandate but to no avail. Even if some workers (especially older employees who have endured job stress for twenty-five or more years) are under a doctor's care, the fast-moving manager may arrange company physicals to certify that her employees can work the required overtime. However, this procedure usually backfires when workers ask their personal physicians how many overtime hours they can work and still maintain their health. In most cases, the company doctor certifies everyone in the department as being able to work the required number of overtime hours, while personal employee physicians (objectively and uncoached) counter that move by stating that fewer and even zero overtime hours should be clocked by their patients!
- ↪ Give top-level management the impression that the manager's department is really dedicated to a particular project and she is a real comer.

Not surprisingly, if management misuses the overtime game, the trust gap between worker and management classes usually widens.

The Popularity Game

Self-promotion can extend from the work environment into such areas as the kind of car you drive, the clothes you wear, the schools your children attend, the address of your home, and so on. All these things can project the illusion that you are extremely successful, for success breeds success, even if you are financed to the hilt.

Unfortunately, you may soon learn that working with your nose to the grindstone and doing a good job, day in and day out, often doesn't cut it in today's large companies. If you do this, the first thing that may occur is that somebody else may try to usurp your popularity for doing good work by taking partial or even full credit for your efforts because he knows you are too busy to attend the meetings where recognition is distributed. Even your manager might not know this is happening until an external sign, such as an award or promotion, ends up in the lap of a sideline player. What the sideline employee decided long ago is that the perception others have of your efforts is what counts, not the act of actually doing something. So, the promotion of your accomplishments (both real and imagined) can take precedence over the act of actually working hard every day at doing your job. This self-promotion becomes all-consuming to the ambitious sideline employee.

How do sideline players succeed at this popularity game? First, they make themselves available to get on the *exposure ride* meaning meetings, travel, and so on. This of course means they have less time to do anything that can be measured. The dialog that occurs on telephones can't be measured, and neither can the dialog that occurs in meetings, in airports, and at the coffee machine. In fact, they can twist most verbal dialog to their advantage. And they never write anything down because this could become a future liability.

Second, sideline players popularize themselves by pitching other people's work as if it were their own. Real workers usually don't like to pitch their accomplishments to others (especially higher-ups) because it takes time away from doing something real. This is unfortunate because sideline players are more than willing to step in and perform this perceived unpleasant task. In fact real workers often come to depend on sideline players to buffer these non-work activities from the real workers' daily lives. Consequently, more often than not, others see Sam Sideline as the originator of Walt Worker's accomplishments.

Another tactic sideline players use to promote themselves is to be on the distribution lists for all the written communication done by working employees. By constantly reading about the efforts of others, they can project the appearance of in-depth knowledge. The fact that Sam Sideline uses new words, concepts, and so on in discussions makes it appear that Sam is one terrific employee, especially to superiors.

An atmosphere of being extremely busy serves the individual striving for popularity well. Fellow workers marvel at such an individual's endurance. This busy profile can range from taking trips out of town to going to local meetings, to attending management briefings. Notice that none of these activities involves measurable work. However, this fact is often lost in the excitement of the race for the title of most popular employee, a title that easily extrapolates into most promotable employee.

The Electronic Communication Game

In large companies, your reputation can be greatly enhanced by the perception you project through work-related communication. In today's business world, e-mail, electronic document interchange, web sites, shared servers, and so on can contain information that you control.

E-mail is an especially useful tool in this endeavor. First, it allows you to state your viewpoint through the contents of memos. Second, you get to define who receives the e-mail communication. Third, you can e-mail memos to people who do not show up on any distribution list (a blind copy list). As the originator of a memo that documents the agreements reached in a meeting, your way of thinking prevails simply because you control the memo's content. This of course may be a conscious or unconscious happening. You need no authorization to send e-mail to anyone, so you may send your memo to important individuals in the company whom you may never even get to meet. You also get to control the *when* and *why* of e-mail distributions. By frequently transmitting communication, you give the perception that you are always on top of things. All this interchange, of course, detracts from the time you spend doing real work, but some people can and do make a career out of the e-mail bonanza.

Generating electronic documents is a boon to people who are good at written communication. Product specifications, customer manuals for products, and so on can bypass the traditional bottleneck of a publication department. During a performance review with management, you can point to documents you created, and you will be identified as the expert regarding the document's content. With today's computer tools, you can include the work of others in your document simply by referencing the names of their computer files. This aspect can make you appear highly productive, and the original contributors will feel elated that you included their written words. Large documents often result from such computer tools, and to some, the larger the document, the more impressive it is.

A web site that you control as a repository for information about particular subjects offers the opportunity to further enhance the impression that you are the authority regarding the web site's content. In reality, others may contribute the information; however, you will probably be identified as the prime mover simply by owning that means of communication. Even if your web site is simply an index to other sites that contain the actual information, your site will still gain notoriety within the company, and your efforts will be highly valued.

The Forecasting Game

In large corporations, proposals for new products and services undergo a practice referred to as *forecasting* (or more commonly, the *business case*). In effect, a prediction is made indicating some type of return (usually monetary) that a particular proposal would add to the company's coffers. Returns can also come in the forms of market penetration (in anticipation of more long-term profits), experience, recognition, and so on. This whole procedure of forecasting is deemed necessary because if large amounts of money, people, and time are consumed working on a project, that effort needs to yield a handsome return that cannot be achieved elsewhere.

Small businesses are not nearly so sophisticated. They tend to do things that are justified by gut feelings or that are simply interesting. Their strategy seems to be to introduce something in the marketplace and see what happens. The consequences of failure are not nearly as great as those of a corporate forecast endeavor. In this manner, new things can appear that would never surface from a large organization. This phenomenon would have you believe that innovation is the property of small organizations, when what may actually occur, at times, is that a small company develops a product that was once the brainchild of someone employed by a large corporation. In reality, innovation in big companies is stilled quite often for lack of a business case. The biggest turnoff that a proponent of something new can experience is to hear the phrase, "What's the business case?" Corporate management doesn't budge without a business case. The forecast distillation process can give real power to those few individuals who delve into this magic art of calculating the future. The savvy employee should learn to use company-sanctioned filters, like the forecast, to his own advantage.

The actual art of forecasting involves assumptions, extrapolations, and other machinations that are merely good guesses of the future. Experience reveals that forecasters seldom take a fall when their predictions are proven to be way off base. For overestimating a forecast, a simple retort of "The market conditions changed" usually blunts most criticism. This phrase is supposed to rebut any responsibility for a product's failure. When a forecaster underestimates a forecast, everyone is simply elated. The forecaster may even gain some status simply because the company is making more money than it expected. In other lines of work, an individual would be chastised for such gross inaccuracies. Not so in the forecasting game.

The Game of Touching the Bases

Ever wonder why progress sometimes seems unjustly thwarted in a large enterprise? Well, large corporations are composed of many divisions, and sometimes these units find themselves competing with each other because of a lack of communication. Large companies often will resort to almost anything to avoid the stigma of having "a lack of communication," which many of them consider the worst of all sins. Yet management often pays homage to such sacred cows without fully understanding the undesirable ramifications: Communication practiced in excess can be a bottleneck, and lengthy procedures can flourish under the guise of communication.

One of these procedures is called the game of *touching the bases.* Briefly, this game requires that certain new or extended activities need to obtain the approval of any and all affected company operating units to avoid potential encroachment. On the surface, this looks OK. In practice, it is easily abused. One of the most efficient ways to perform this communication would be to invite the affected parties to partake in an open discussion. The duration of such an event might only take an hour or two, and any arrived-at understandings would have the blessings of the participants. However, the more politically advantaged approach is for management to hold a private meeting with each of the affected parties in advance of the formal discussion. This tactic is meant to convey the utmost respect, and at the same time it minimizes any disagreements because each can be handled with a personal touch. For example, several affected parties may have the same problem, and management may think the problem's importance would be exaggerated in an open discussion. In a private, one-on-one mode, however, the magnification of any joint disagreement can be deflected if not eliminated. The favorable conclusion of a touch-the-bases game is a needless meeting with a predetermined conclusion.

Failure to touch all the bases before the main event is a serious breach of management conduct that can be potentially disastrous. In such a case, offended parties may feel they have the right to critique anything and everything. Remember that some critics derive satisfaction from killing something, just as doers derive satisfaction from achieving something. However, a deliberate snub may actually work in favor of a functional manager who has a hidden agenda. For example, sometimes managers appear to champion projects, but in reality they may have been forced into this dilemma because of a favor owed to others, a perceived lack of initiative by their peers, or whatever. The point is: They may not be believers.

In this case, the manager's use of a *sacrificial lamb* as the meeting's facilitator or presenter can be most advantageous. In its implementation, a sacrificial lamb (or surrogate champion) is chosen to present the case for doing or not doing something in the combined meeting. Then the snubbed detractors usually begin their onslaught, as the manager expected. The discussion begins to sway to the negative, and this is when the sacrificial lamb's manager gracefully shifts his support away from the perceived mistake. He succeeds in derailing something that he considered doubtful while not enduring the verbal abuse targeted at the surrogate.

Warning signs that you are becoming a sacrificial lamb include being chosen to attend, organize, or present at a meeting to which you would not normally be invited. Remember that unfavorable notoriety has a way of following you around in your career. Avoid this unpleasantness if possible. If avoidance is not possible, remind your manager, afterward, that he owes you.

It is easy to see that this game takes a lot of time. What began as a courtesy can attain the status of a full-fledged, time-wasting, communication-redundant—but politically suave—tactic.

Financial Games

When you complete a business trip, it is good practice to fill out an expense form as quickly as possible so as not to forget reimbursable items, such as parking fees, toll charges, currency exchange rates for foreign travel, and so on. Furthermore, most all companies have expense guidelines for rental cars, hotel prices, meal charges, airline tickets, phone calls, and so on. You name it, and the company usually has a guideline for it.

Financial analysts, accountants, and the like often seem to delight in declaring all kinds of restraints on spending. The trouble is that, although the goal is to keep expenses to a fair and reasonable amount, the guidelines can unknowingly encourage frivolous spending as a type of revenge for some ridiculous guideline. For example, if the company says to deduct mileage normally spent driving to/from work from the round-trip mileage claimed for driving to/from the airport, the irritated employee's reaction may be to hire a taxi/limousine (each way). The company will usually reimburse this expense (several times the amount of using the employee's own car) without question. Similarly, some accountants may say you cannot deduct the cost of your lunch during a business trip if there is a company cafeteria at the visited site. This guideline only encourages employees to spend more on dinner than they normally would.

The expense of moving is another area where accountants may actually increase costs by the restraints they place on employees who are being transferred. An example of an illogical moving-expense restraint is when a company will not pay to have a grandfather clock properly boxed to eliminate damage in transit. However, the company will pay for damage to the clock, to get it into running order at the new location. Similarly, shipping more than two cars is sometimes not reimbursed, so the employee ends up driving the third car to her new job location and is reimbursed for mileage, hotels, and meals. This expense can easily exceed the amount the company would have spent on airfare and shipping of the car by a large amount.

Penny-wise, Dollar-foolish Games

A company absorbs many costs not directly related to producing and selling goods and services. Among these expenses is the ordinary maintenance of a company's physical plant facilities. These maintenance services are usually subcontracted for a number of reasons. For example, a policy of outsourcing can help a company avoid paying maintenance workers medical and retirement benefits enjoyed by the company's regular employees. If the workers for a subcontracted service do not receive coverage or receive less than adequate coverage, this does not detract from the reputation of a corporation that is respected for treating its employees fairly. So often the strategy is to get the cheapest subcontractor while maintaining minimum standards. This policy appears OK at first glance but has led to some practices that detract from this stated goal. The implementation of maintenance services can contain many abuses that actually increase a company's costs.

For example, cleaning services that keep up the appearance of the work environment include running the vacuum cleaner, emptying wastebaskets, washing chalkboards, and so on. The intent is to provide a neat, pleasant atmosphere for the regular employees. People are supposed to be happy and thus more productive. Instead, in pursuit of minimal costs, these services may occur during regular work hours to avoid paying a shift differential. The effect on the regular employees is one of irritation. Individuals may react to the interruptions by walking out of their offices to get cups of coffee, visiting their peer employees who have not yet been invaded, or tolerating the unplanned incursions by pretending they are not disturbed. The net result is that a corporation most likely loses because workers usually resent the intrusions and may either stop working to retaliate or work at reduced levels of efficiency.

Cleaning the restrooms on a scheduled basis is another task that is better handled outside of prime shift. Yet "Temporarily Closed for Cleaning" signs that announce such activity are regularly tolerated with annoyance and displeasure. An employee's immediate reaction to such a sign is usually to look for another restroom so he can return to a productive state. This could involve a journey to another floor or even another building. Such visits cannot be postponed. Again, the company is trading lost employee time for a low-cost subcontractor.

Undoubtedly, filling the vending machines must occur on a periodic basis, but it would be better to perform this activity after regular work hours. When machines are filled during prime shift, lines form and trips to other machines compensate for this practice. Again, the employee spends time on unproductive endeavors that he wants to avoid.

In addition, cable wiring (such as that for personal computer connections), office furniture moves, and other less-frequent employee intrusions are also candidates for prime shift. Such things happen infrequently, but they still cause disruptions, such as stringing cable through office ceilings, monopolizing elevators, and crowding hallways (a safety consideration).

Why do these practices continue? One reason is that their effect on worker productivity is not directly measurable while the cost of subcontractors is. A myopic management needs to look beyond the obvious.

The Estimating/Commitment Game

A manager's career of monitoring, directing, attending meetings, and so on by its very essence does not lend itself to accurately evaluating what it takes for another employee to accomplish the specifics of an assignment. So, the savvy manager will ask (rather than tell) a chosen employee to make an estimate of what a particular task will take (for example, regarding time schedule, functional content, quality, etc.) before externally committing to anything. Professional employees perform better if they feel a sense of participation in their jobs. The experienced individual making the estimate knows that she will probably be held to her assessment, so she factors in such things as:

- ❧ Handling interruptions regarding questions/problems associated with previous assignments
- ❧ Attending meetings that occur on a regular and irregular basis
- ❧ Determining outside dependencies that affect the completion of the assignment, including such things as training, obtaining additional people, using tools (such as computer resources), and requiring a completed work effort by a peer department
- ❧ Working a normal eight-hour day
- ❧ Being creative

Somehow sick days never make it into a commitment, but they happen just the same.

When the manager receives the estimate, he may add his personal touch to make it politically correct. There is an uncommunicated expectation that he must not embarrass his estimating peers with an overly optimistic projection of what it takes to do a job. For safety's sake, it is always better to overestimate any judgment call. It is not unusual for employee estimates to be doubled or tripled. In a lot of cases, there is a specious correlation of estimate cost to difficulty. Some managers may promote the perception that what they will undertake is highly complex and highly risky. This can serve as an excuse if the estimate-turned-commitment is missed. Also it enhances the reputations of the managers before anything is done simply because of the difficulty perception.

Handing down a dictated estimate (that tells when, what, and how) is a tactic that generally works on inexperienced professional employees. They are eager to please and have not yet learned that it is perfectly acceptable to question (in the form of obtaining a better understanding) the validity of any judgments that may directly affect their future assignments. People who are instructed to follow a dictated estimate usually end up doing what they are told, not what was intended or what is required. It's a kind of subconscious resentment, which can surface in missed schedules and poor quality. The person who inherits a dictated estimate should immediately spend time reviewing any and all commitments. He should voice his disagreement about those that appear shaky. Silence indicates acceptance.

The Work Assignment Game

Now and then, assignments crop up in the workplace that were not factored into anyone's schedule. The manager needs to delegate these tasks to his employees and usually attempts to do so in a diplomatic manner. Instead of telling, he asks an employee if she is not too busy to accept this additional responsibility. Now the employee is faced with a dilemma. If she accepts, she may run the risk of missing other commitments because of an additional task. If she responds negatively, then she may appear to be uncooperative, inflexible, or even a minimal contributor.

The savvy employee should accept the extra assignment with a word of caution to her manager. A simple statement that describes the impact of an added responsibility is usually sufficient. Then the ball is back in the court of the manager. He must make the decision by weighing what his employee told him. This is how the give-and-take manager-employee work assignment procedure is supposed to work.

Unfortunately, what happens does not always conform to this model. For example, inexperienced employees, eager to please, may accept added responsibilities without realizing the new responsibilities can have an adverse effect on their already taxed work load. In managers' rush to find a name to associate with a task, some naive supervisors may be more than happy to accept a no-strings-attached positive response from an employee who wants to please. They hope things will work out and, for a moment, forget their job is to evaluate what employees tell them and come up with their own conclusions about the reasonableness, validity, and doability of the assignment. Nevertheless, once an employee makes a commitment, it usually means she owns the problem and is on the hook to deliver. Entry-level people frequently don't appreciate the seriousness of the commitment procedure. Their reputations are at stake. However, if things don't go as expected, the impulsive manager can end up sharing the blame for missed or late deliverables. Now and then, the playing field is leveled.

Some Management Games That Unfortunately Work

Diversionary Tactics

How can an ambitious manager neutralize the opposition for long periods of time? Sadly, some managers resort to getting people to work on something that is going nowhere. First off, the diversionary assignment needs the blessing of management. Statements such as "The competition is working on this," "It's the wave of the future," and "The company needs this to demonstrate . . ." are difficult to evaluate but are often used to justify some vague task. Even more convincing can be the ability to disguise a proposal in esoteric phrases. Because no one wants to admit that he does not understand what is being proposed, questions that should be asked may remain unspoken, and people may even get assigned to the project. It may take several months before this maneuver is exposed. All the time, the originator of this tactic is free to work on other responsibilities without interference.

Sometimes the project a manager is working on gets into trouble. It could be because of a schedule, capability, or other expectation that was committed in good faith. What to do? Unfortunately, some people in this situation begin to look for other managers who are also floundering and bring the plight of their distraught peers to the attention of the higher-ups. Then, these superiors will sometimes schedule an audit to evaluate the extent of the exposure and potential damage. This activity takes time, which allows the manager with the problem time to fix his own dilemma while others fall further behind. Simultaneously, such a manager preserves the perception that all is well with his assignment. His reputation for spotting potential problems also benefits from this strategy.

Do your best to steer clear of such game playing. Remember your work commitments and do your best to honor them. If you can't, accept responsibility.

The Education Ploy

When the pressure at work gets too intense, some managers may prescribe for themselves a rest on company time. These managers may deem it wise to schedule a few company-sponsored educational classes in advance of a perceived difficulty (they can always be canceled). They prefer educational absences because this diversion enhances others' perception of their desire to improve their capabilities. Besides, they may reason, some crises have a way of resolving themselves without their personal involvement. They can even extend such absences from work by choosing a mode of transportation that is not time efficient. For example, a cross-country trip on a train gives them an extra couple of days away from the office. It also makes them unreachable by phone or other communication.

If you are ever in a situation to receive company-paid education, be grateful for the opportunity and remember your job is to learn, not to waste time.

The Arabesque Maneuver

Pressure to participate in a strategic company endeavor can be the cause of great anxiety for the manager who does not believe in such a venture (he may support an alternative). He may even be told that he needs to get up to speed to make up for his procrastinating attitude regarding the endeavor. Some managers handle this situation in a less-than-aboveboard manner. First, they may give the appearance of cooperation by agreeing to participate in discussions with those "in the know." Then they may direct all their department members to meet with these knowledgeable people. Next, after a suitable time period allowing for an exchange of information, they may declare that their people are *leading the discussions* and they, as managers, are therefore withdrawing from further meetings because their people appear to be more advanced, more in the know.

Refrain from such sneaky tactics. They have a way of resurfacing later in your career, in some form, and eroding your self-esteem.

Conclusion

Most employees engage in work activities without appreciating the fact that they are involved in a variety of gaming activities that occur daily in the workplace. To survive the tactics employed by your peers, look for signs identifying people and conditions that provide a breeding ground for such maneuvers. Develop your own insight into *situations* so that you recognize when things of this type can and do happen. How can you win if you don't know the rules? Besides, this developed trait can make working more exciting and less routine.

The Meeting Phenomenon
~ or ~
Wake Me When It's Time to Work

The larger the corporation, the greater the number of meetings. Small companies simply cannot afford the luxury of having their employees waste valuable time verbalizing about topics that are better addressed by the written hand or by informal gatherings in someone's office or even at the vending machine. It is a sad fact of corporate life that some individuals make their livings attending meetings.

Meeting Background

In any large company, it is extremely important to attend as many meetings as possible. When management states that an exceptionally productive employee "needs more exposure" if he expects to be promoted, this usually has an immediate impact on that employee's work habits. Instead of concentrating on doing the job for which he is paid, he looks at the work calendars of important people so he will know what meetings are forthcoming. In this way, he is able to invite himself to all the right places so he can become known to the big players. In large corporations, it is an accepted phenomenon that meetings are necessary even though everyone knows they can be an excuse to avoid doing any measurable work. Meetings result in shared decisions that can further extend the careers of the incompetent. The employee soon discovers that he must learn *meeting protocol* if he is to become adept at playing the meeting game. When playing the meeting game, you should be aware of several rules:

- It is important to comment on the happenings within any meeting. Certain phrases are always valid and sound impressive regardless of the meeting's objective or content. For example, if an individual says, "We need to escalate this problem to higher-level management," it immediately gives the impression that the employee knows upper management, understands the importance of the problem, and is an individual of action—even though that employee may not have the faintest idea what's going on. He is able to detect the right moment to say such an important-sounding phrase after attending a couple of meetings where others are practicing the same game as he. The right moment can be during a presentation when there is disagreement about what a speaker is actually saying. The ambitious employee doesn't even have to understand the differences—only that there is disagreement. Other catchy phrases such as "The schedule is too tight," "What does marketing think?" and even "We need to schedule another meeting with the right people" also appear insightful.
- One's seating position at a meeting is of utmost importance. In large gatherings where there is a central conference table with limited chairs, there is usually a second tier of seating positioned against the walls. These seats are meant for less-important attendees. Usually, only the important people occupy conference table chairs, but if you arrive early, you can secure one of these valued positions and thus be identified as a major player without ever saying anything of value.
- Be sure to position yourself near the dominant personality or near other attendees who represent the accepted viewpoint, even though doing so may conflict with other meeting protocols such as making sure you obtain a conference table seat. This gives the illusion that you are associated with the people likely to win any confrontation that occurs within the meeting.
- Always be sure any assignments that occur within the meeting are delegated to others. At all costs, avoid taking on any real work assignment. This can severely detract from your time allotted for attending other important meetings.
- Meetings of contention in which the losing faction will be clearly recognized may result in the use of a *sacrificial lamb*, who may or

may not be aware of what is happening during the course of the meeting. Here's how this works: During the meeting, seasoned game players who recognize the possibility of a losing effort begin shifting their positions to some unsuspecting individual so they may appear as both winners and perceptive meeting participants who identify the real culprit. Comments such as "I've always maintained. . . ," "At the last meeting you said. . . ," "Did you say. . .?" and "That's impossible" indicate that a position shift is coming and a sacrificial lamb is being targeted. Watch out: No rules isolate you from taking the fall during a meeting, and the attack may even come from members of your own department.

Regularly Scheduled Meetings

Meetings can consume much time and sometimes yield almost no payback. The number of meeting rooms in a building also tends to accelerate the need for such gatherings by fostering the perception that meetings are always necessary, good, and part of the corporate environment. This notion can exist even at the lowest worker level. To be invited to a meeting is considered a mark of status by the naive and uninformed. Types of meetings may include departmental meetings, functional area meetings, mission meetings, physical site meetings, and so on.

Department managers feel obligated to host gatherings to keep everyone informed about the activities of each member of the department and to discuss other topics of general interest, such as how the department plays a role in the big corporate picture. On the surface this sounds like a good idea. However, this puts pressure on individuals to recall all their activities (they will be called on to describe them in some detail) since the last meeting so that others may benefit from this information. In reality, *meeting people* sometimes make up things or embellish their work efforts in order to have something to say when their turn occurs. The *really busy people* want the meeting to end as soon as possible because it is taking them away from productive work. Often, people who have no real work responsibilities that can be measured become *long-winded orators* when it comes time to enumerate their accomplishments. Such an individual usually ends up discussing the fact that he is involved in some vague, abstract, and yes, immeasurable assignment. It sounds important because most participants have no idea of either the subject matter or its content (especially if he has just made it up). Some managers present may incorrectly perceive that the long-winded person taking up so much time borders on the genius level because of his expertise at the wordsmith game and the complicated ramifications of his assignment, which only he comprehends. To ask a probing question would be too risky for such a manager because it might sound as if the questioner is simply not acquainted with the subject. These departmental meetings have a way of occurring on a regularly scheduled basis, thus furthering the notion that real work should take a backseat to this perceived gala communication event.

Area meetings and other meetings of a scope greater than departmental sound really important because multiple departments are involved and participants get the opportunity to become known to others who may help their careers. In reality, many of these meetings occur because they make the host look like she is keeping everyone informed about what's happening. She may even think this is the most important aspect of her job requirement. Really busy workers either don't care to know what's going on or are too busy to attend such a gathering. The content of these meetings can easily be learned from other attendees or by a subsequent meeting summary notice. So why do people attend? The reason is simple. To see, be seen, and avoid real work. For some people, attending area meetings is a favorite way of furthering their careers without the baggage of doing real work.

Meeting Customs

When a corporation designates a number of rooms for meetings, it extends an invitation to potentially unproductive endeavors. (In environments where real work is being accomplished, there is often a scarcity—or even total absence—of meeting rooms.) The names of these meeting places are sometimes elevated to titles such as conference rooms or executive suites to give the illusion of importance. For a company to have such places is like spreading honey for the ants because some employees believe that attending meetings beats working.

Consequently, a whole *meeting culture* can develop within a company. Computer tools such as electronic calendars further enhance the importance of meetings. In such a culture, it soon becomes accepted practice to view other employees' calendars to find out what meetings your adversary may be planning or simply for reasons of social contact. You can electronically reserve a meeting room anywhere within a company, even at different plant sites. The most coveted rooms come with a view and are lavishly decorated. Of course, meeting rooms with leather-covered chairs and walnut conference tables can only be scheduled for high-level meetings. In fact, a conference room pecking order can be observed as the covering for chairs becomes more elaborate—coverings range from leather and cloth to wood or simply plastic.

In a meeting culture, managers sometimes enhance their egos and gain status by sending notices requesting one-on-one meetings with their employees, even though they may sit three steps (office door to office door) away. These managers view such tools as elevating to their stature. Employees can't just knock on a door and discuss a problem; a meeting has to be scheduled for such a dialog to take place. Not only that, but these managers may even tell their secretaries to set up such a meeting. Eventually, people become so accustomed to attending such time wasters that if there is no meeting to attend, they become uneasy because they have forgotten how to do anything real. Old-time communication techniques such as the telephone, a chance encounter at the coffee machine, or even just dropping in a neighbor's office to discuss a point can become obsolete because such methods lack the political credibility associated with group decisions. This meeting culture erodes any initiative of creative individuals.

Meeting Agendas

There are various reasons to hold a meeting, and the participants have a large influence on the way it progresses. Many individuals look upon a meeting as an opportunity to gain exposure to happenings in other areas of the company. Others use it to flaunt their knowledge about various subjects to impress their fellow workers and especially the management responsible for their next promotion. These two agendas are the most common side effects that occur at these gatherings. However, there is another less-obvious occurrence known as the hidden agenda. The meeting itself is the excuse to gather people together, but the collection of participants can cause the discussion topics to wander far from the official reason for holding the meeting. Hidden agendas include (but are not limited to) the following two types:

> ↬ Agenda to embarrass the presenter
> This hidden agenda meeting usually starts with innocent questions to which the meeting's originators already know the answers. It quickly progresses to more embarrassing topics that are outside the expertise of the speaker. Unknowingly, the speaker tries to accommodate the meeting's participants but ends up either yielding to individuals who are proficient in such topics or admitting that she does not know the answers to the questions.

Immediately the attendees perceive that the speaker possesses no in-depth knowledge about her own meeting. The speaker should have recognized what was happening and steered the discussion back to the original topic. She should have said that these other topics should more properly be the subject of another meeting.

↦ Agenda to kill the product
The objective of the meeting may be to discuss the progress of putting out a new company product. Instead, the meeting's detractors see it as an opportunity to say such negative things as "The forecast says this product should be killed," "There are too many legal problems to announce the product at this time," and "The quality of this product is too inadequate to announce it to the marketplace."

Meeting Room Consequences

Meetings tend to be dominated by individuals possessing good verbal skills, who can manipulate the spoken word to their advantage. Equally important are the confrontational abilities of the participants. Loud noises, verbal abuse, statements about someone's parental heritage, and so on are all meant to intimidate those less experienced at the meeting game. As a result, others in attendance—or even those absent from such gatherings—often end up with work to do. How do you combat such behavior? One effective strategy is to offer to record the occurrences that transpire. More than likely, your request will be granted because this necessitates real work. Why is this technique effective? Simple—you get to put your slant on everything that takes place. The following examples point out some of the advantages of serving in this capacity:

1. The recording-of-the-minutes appointee gets to make up (or alter) the distribution list.
   ↦ You can add names as best serves your purpose. A blind carbon copy list can inform potential allies without making others aware of this act. An explicitly added name can panic others into believing you may have an upper management protector.
   ↦ You can subtract names from the distribution list. This ploy delays correspondence to your opponents until you are notified of your error. By that time, the effect of the

meeting's minutes has already begun. This ruse also lessens the perceived importance of the person you deleted.

2. You become somewhat of a default authority on the subjects discussed at the meeting. Questions, clarifications, revisions, and so on all pass through your hands. If the meeting addressed a subject you want to become associated with, then you have already demonstrated your acuity. Alternately, if you are good at the written word, you may even get invited to other meetings, where your skills can further enhance your reputation.

3. The insertion (or deletion) of selected words/phrases can alter the degree of commitment that was agreed to at the meeting. This can be used as you see fit. For example, adding the word *projected* to delivery dates implies that they are good guesses but not firm dates.

How to Run a Good Meeting

The ingredients of successful meetings begin by using some common sense. First, not everyone should be able to call a meeting. Some sort of filter should be utilized to shut off this distraction. If permission to convene an assembly of employees is granted to someone, then that person should state the expected output up front. If this can't be communicated, then why hold such an event?

Next, remember that each employee's time is valuable, so keep the meeting as brief as possible. Don't get comfortable in a room containing plush surroundings. Using an empty office usually ensures a short duration. Remember that people's attention spans decrease the longer they have to be in attendance. Individuals tend to get anxiety because of time spent away from their regular work assignments. Meetings should be the exception to the everyday work experience.

All meetings need a chairperson who never loses focus of what the meeting is supposed to attain. In this light, extraneous discussion should be recognized and dealt with accordingly. Another important responsibility of this person is to shut off discussion when it becomes abusive and personal. Even extended technical discussions are better handled in an exchange that includes only participants who understand the technical terms. A seasoned chairperson will ensure that work assignments are passed out to attendees, to bring some sort of closure on the points raised in a meeting.

Home Turf Meetings

Multi-site corporations that work on large, complicated projects generally require the participation of various locations because the nature of the undertaking is just too big for a single location. This may also occur because the work load needs to be distributed to keep their skilled work force employed. Such a distribution of work aimed at a coordinated end game necessitates the use of individuals who interface with the various locations to maintain open, clear, concise communication. People employed in this capacity wield much influence because they know (or are supposed to know) what the other guys are doing. This effort results in many face-to-face meetings, as well as formal documentation, describing exactly who does what. Experience teaches that intracompany verbal agreements can be massaged, manipulated, interpreted, extrapolated, and twisted to gain an advantage when things don't go as planned. Partners can easily become adversaries. In large companies, it is crucial to maintain an image of meeting commitments, for this is one important way employee performance is judged.

The location of any meeting is extremely important, for it gives the host built-in advantages that may not be readily apparent. First, the fact that individuals travel to a given location signifies automatic respect, tribute, and esteem. Right off, the participant from the host meeting site enjoys the benefits of a presumed leadership role in any negotiations. Familiar surroundings also remove any sense of anxiety and uncertainty. Mundane things, like knowing when the company cafeteria opens and closes, the location of restrooms, and the location of the coffee machines, give the owner of such knowledge an automatic sense of authority.

The degree of a meeting's formality can be enhanced with catered refreshments, plush meeting facilities with wood furniture, paneled walls, and windows with views. The amount of importance that is associated with such surroundings can thus be controlled by such symbols of correctness and pomp. The host additionally enjoys the advantage of being able to call in any local, available expert to support his viewpoint. The visitor, on the other hand, must rely on her personal knowledge or on that of her fellow travelers, who have their own interests at stake.

The pressure to reach some level of understanding mounts as the length of the meeting progresses. Visitors are more willing to compromise as their return trip home gets closer. It is easy to tire of hotels, dining out, and an unfamiliar environment. The host surely understands this advantage, and so do most out-of-town attendees. Going home without any agreement gives people an empty feeling and even a feeling of failure. Everyone needs to feel some degree of accomplishment occurred. The host can hold out longer because he already knows he will be going home every evening.

Consequently, management versed in the political games of working for a big company clearly wants to establish its own location as the meeting site for any multi-location project. Such a role provides immediate notoriety without doing anything. This aspect appeals to people who require visibility.

Conclusion

Be aware that the meeting culture is a fact of life in large corporations. Only experience will teach you which meetings are beneficial and which are held to perpetuate the illusion of progress. Avoid feelings of emptiness that linger after a particularly worthless gathering of fellow workers.

Office Survival
Information

~ or ~

How to Avoid Falling for
Hooks, Lines, and Stinkers

Some things happen at work that the unknowing may interpret in a manner that is entirely unrelated to the actual happening. This chapter will attempt to help you read between the lines (when appropriate) to gain a balanced understanding of office occurrences.

Special Assignment

It stands to reason that managers who make big mistakes at work will likely be removed from their positions of authority. This action usually takes place as quietly as possible because the company doesn't want to give the impression that one of the good old boys is no longer on the team. Rarely will the company publicly say that Joe Manager was at fault. Instead, such deposed individuals may be placed in new positions that have little real work to perform. When this happens, an announcement may be posted on the company's bulletin boards, saying that Joe Manager is on *special assignment.* Now, if you witness such a situation, pay close attention because the term *special assignment* often means the named individual is in a temporary holding pattern looking for a new job either within or outside the company. This form of employment has also become widely known as the *penalty box.*

For example, let's say Joe Manager is on special assignment with his new title, manager of advanced intergalactic planning. This grandiose title sounds impressive to the outside world, but in reality it means "manager of nothing." If the deposed manager has a godfather, he has nothing to worry about. He still receives his paycheck and other perks (stock options) while serving out his time. (In fact, some managers look forward to being penalized as a time of relaxation.) He is relieved of the day-to-day pressures of a demanding job. But what is missing is the power he once enjoyed.

When management determines that a defrocked individual has been penalized enough, he may be brought out of obscurity and given a job of some importance. When his new assignment is announced, you will probably never hear about the unfortunate incident that initiated his term in the penalty box. Usually, only his achievements are mentioned. Perhaps this is how it should be. For if people are never given second chances, then no one will ever take a risk that may result in failure.

Vending Machine Frustrations

Whenever it is time for a coffee break, don't be surprised if you must stand in line to spend your money. In some companies, top executives attempt to discourage coffee breaks by limiting the coffee machines to one per floor or, worse yet, one per every other floor. One coffee machine per floor of hundreds of workers is simply not equipped to service people on a timely basis. Imagine the time lost when an employee must take an elevator to have a cup of coffee. (This really happens. This is being penny-wise and dollar-foolish, as the saying goes.) When you finally reach the coffee machine, then the machine may not work, or even worse, it may be out of cups or void of cream/sugar. Companies should pay attention to these details because such frustrations can divert an employee's attention away from work for a much longer period than the average coffee break.

Most companies recognize that employees appreciate small things, like free coffee—especially because they may be working long hours without benefit of compensation (as does a salaried worker). Only the truly miserly companies charge for such amenities. These companies even charge an extra nickel for a paper cup. (By the way, most organizations make a small profit off the vending machine proceeds.)

In some companies, when a vending machine eats your money, you must fill out a form to get your money back, identifying the malfunction, the location of the machine, its serial number, and so on. By doing this, you are doing the field diagnosis job for the vending company. Some vendors may even have the nerve to tell you that they would have to increase the cost of a cup of coffee if you did not help them control costs in this way, but you must understand that your company has given the vendor a monopoly of this business within its boundaries. Only competition will awaken the sloppy vendor. If you do the paperwork right, you may get a refund in a couple of weeks. But most people can't be bothered to do all the paperwork, especially if they are conscientious workers wanting to get back to their offices and continue working.

Recognition Pitfalls

Occasionally companies honor their employees by hosting events for both the employee and spouse. These recognition gatherings are meant to emotionally compensate the employees and their partners for the long hours of separation they endure because of the needs of the business. Unfortunately, the relevance of these happenings and the intended morale boost are easily diluted if the elapsed time between project end and the recognition event is significant. In some cases, a coordinated gala episode can cause time lapses of several years.

Such elaborate affairs for a multi-division, multi-location corporation usually take place in a large city that is easily accessible. This necessitates overnight lodging for out-of-town employees. Because of the large number of attendees, you may be told beforehand that the company has booked reservations at multiple hotels. If this is the case, be prepared for a disparity between the quality of hotels. The company may explain that employees who traveled the farthest get to stay in the best hotel because their chances of visiting this particular city (for, say, sightseeing) are less than the chances of those individuals who live closer. This seems pretty understandable and fair. However, sometimes you may discover later that recognized employees from nearby corporate locations (as opposed to not-so-nearby plant sites) also were given accommodations in the best hotel. The disparity is likely not because of the degree of recognition (such as a monetary award) but rather because of the pecking order prevalent in most big companies. But companies should take note: Educated workers possess a keen smell for inequality. Admiration for the company declines with each violation of impartiality.

The gala affair usually begins with a sit-down dinner. But be prepared: Companies often select seating partners for you. This way, Jill Employee from the East Coast gets to meet Mike Employee from the West Coast. Peer acquaintances with whom you have toiled long hours (and gained mutual respect) may be seated at other tables. If this happens, you may be tempted to get angry. After all, you may reason, the company has failed to appreciate the fact that a recognition celebration has a more momentous, meaningful effect if it is done in the presence of friends, not strangers. But be careful not to let your anger take control of you, or you may spend the evening seething rather than enjoying the gala happening.

The Dual Ladder

When you begin professional employment at a large company, you will probably be told two career paths are open to you. One is management, and the other is technical. Either one is fine to choose, as long as you know about some key differences between the two when making your decision.

For starters, the levels available for management promotion usually exceed those available to technical workers. Administrators can be elevated to a first, second, third, fourth, fifth, and even sixth (and so on) management level, each with accompanying benefits, such as enhanced retirement plans, stock options, bonus money, travel amenities (for example, first-class airline and hotel accommodations), varying incentive plans, salary increases, and so on. Also, administrators' office space, views, and accompanying decorations are oftentimes more lavish than those allotted to technical workers, even if the employees are at the same pay grade level. On the flip side, technical workers usually get to enjoy hands-on work more often than those who choose the managerial route, and to many people, this more than makes up for any perks they may miss out on.

Euphemisms Used in Canceled Projects

Now and then, company projects get killed because the company comes to a startling realization that what is being developed is not competitive. You may suspect this is happening when you hear phrases like "The market is not ready for such an innovative product," "Market conditions have changed," "International requirements dictate that we need to re-examine the product's impact," and even "A shift in company priorities mandates the reassignment of resources to other projects." When you hear such euphemisms, it likely means the company is watering down the truth to keep from admitting it made a mistake.

But why should companies feel like they must pretend to be invincible? Everyone makes mistakes. Instead, injecting some realism into the running of a large company would have a positive effect on the regular employees. After all, people are more educated than ever before, so a dose of honesty would probably do some good.

Veteran employees know the symptoms of projects that are on the verge of cancellation. Numerous meetings, charts, justifications, analyses, trips to headquarters, and so on seem to ensure a project's demise. Points can be scored with high-level executives by individuals assigned to these tasks. Occasionally, when a product cancellation is brought to the attention of higher management by the project's manager himself, then all is forgiven. As most soon learn, it's better to be open and honest before your intracompany adversaries tell on you.

The Staffing Phenomenon

A look at how the staffing of projects occurs within a large corporation provides an opportunity to appreciate why it can take so long to accomplish anything in such organizations. Projects can fail even before the real work starts if:

- The company ignores the background experience of individuals selected to lead within the organization. In such a case, a mismatch occurs between a leader's background and the department she is hired to manage (for example, a former marketer managing a manufacturing department). If she is high enough in the organization, then her efforts usually don't have any effect, and projects can succeed in spite of her position. However, if she is placed in a first-line management position, her tenure can be disastrous.
- The company fills both technical and management positions with individuals simply because these people are available. Often, people are available to accept jobs because no one else wants to hire them. Then when competent people are finally placed within the organization, dissension occurs because it's too late to change the technical direction and the good people want out.
- The people in charge of hiring are repaying friends for past favors. This is especially dangerous because of the loss of objectivity and the tendency among such selected individuals to become "yes men" to the higher-ups.
- The people in charge of hiring choose individuals who will please the higher-ups to gain favor. This could range from fast trackers to friends of important managers within the company.

֍ The company acquires as many people as possible to staff a project. This ensures the perceived importance of the project within the company but usually slows things down. Good communication is the first ingredient of success that suffers. The tasks of workers become so specialized that the big picture becomes fuzzy, and design/implementation trade-offs that could have been handled without fanfare now require regularly scheduled meetings, international teleconferences, and management decisions about matters that really should be the domain of real workers. Because the organization becomes so large, more procedures are put in place to handle the communication problem. Of course, this leads to people having to document a lot of stuff that should be handled verbally, and the real work suffers.

The Worldwide Dog-and-Pony Show

Opportunities for worldwide travel often surface when the time comes for the company to popularize a new direction for one or more of its product lines. To people skilled in the art of giving pitches to corporate executives, this often represents a career enhancement window because of the personal exposure possible in large corporations. After particularly successful meetings, these pitchmen become identified with the new direction. However, sometimes they can become so intoxicated with their new notoriety and power that they make up product commitments and delivery schedules that have no relation to reality. This creates added pressure on the actual workers because soon the dates become cast in concrete.

From there, the pitch often takes on the aura of a circus by providing executives with entertainment, as well as excuses to attend such briefings. Trips to both U.S. coasts become routine, as well as European and Asian tours. The frequent flier mileage begins to accrue rapidly, and the pitchmen are soon traveling first class because of the upgrades airlines hand out to favored passengers who seem to go everywhere. Other perks, such as hotel accommodations and new car rentals, are all upgraded. Consequently, some pitchmen caught up in the worldwide dog-and-pony show see themselves as the visionaries of the company and act accordingly.

This circus can last for years until it comes time to actually deliver what the pitchmen promised. Then it dawns on those who sponsored the project that it has many failings, such as not meeting customer requirements, performing poorly, not meeting delivery dates, and being highly unreliable.

The Unsuspecting Entry-Level Employee

As a new hire, you will probably become aware that the company has both an administrative and technical career path for most company functions. However, the administrative (management) slots are usually reserved for individuals who have already worked a number of years for the company. To soften the impact of this information, however, the company may lead you to believe that most everything (with rare exceptions) is equal for a manager attaining a certain pay grade and a technical worker attaining the identical classification. This sounds great, but as a new college graduate you have not yet mastered the art of reading between the lines of such nice-sounding statements.

Surprise difference No. 1 may be that the pay equality is valid only up to a certain level. Although senior technical positions may be available in all large corporations, the number of such positions is usually small when compared with the number of people who manage at those levels. This numerical difference occurs (says management) because business expansion/changes create the need for more managers. It's amusing that expansion/changes never seem to create the need for a like amount of senior professional workers.

Surprise difference No. 2 may be that the opportunities for career advancement into positions of significant importance and responsibility are reserved only for management types. Thus, if you choose to be a non-manager, you may place a ceiling on your career advancement. If money and power are important to you, then management is usually the best career path to follow.

New employees are usually hired because management can easily point them to work that cannot possibly be accomplished by the present staff. So, as new employees are hired, the most challenging (a euphemism for risky) and directly measurable assignments are given to them. Most seasoned employees learned long ago that risk is not well rewarded and safety rests in time-tested tasks. Experience also taught veterans that it is better to be a member of a support function—such as a test, documentation, or planning group—allied with a development group that is on the firing line.

Ultimately, the phenomenon that occurs is that entry-level employees in large corporations are doing most of the front-line important work, and they must compete with established workers in smaller companies where everyone is used to taking risks. This erodes the advantage once held by large companies because new services and product development are in the hands of relatively new hires, who must compete with veterans in smaller organizations.

Most large companies pay overtime to entry-level employees for additional hours they spend on the job. This entices them to work hard and long hours as the money keeps rolling in. However, soon management recognizes that if these hard-working new employees were promoted into exempt positions, the company would benefit because *exempt* means "excluded from earning overtime pay." Caught in the dilemma of accepting or declining a small raise for a promotion at the expense of eliminating overtime pay, most new employees succumb to the promotion because of status and a desire to remain in management's good graces.

Advantages of Being an Entry-Level Employee

New employees, especially recent graduates, can profit from their inexperience in a number of ways. They come from learning environments, so they are therefore used to encountering situations that require analysis, deduction, abstract thinking, and other traits associated with an inquiring intellect. Their minds are not yet crowded with baggage that can detract from unbiased thinking. As new employees, they are not yet bothered with regularly scheduled meetings. Office politics and other time-consuming games that detract from the goal of gaining experience have not yet become a part of their daily regimen. They are left alone to just do their jobs. New hires should take advantage of this unencumbered state by doing real things. Numerous inquiries from entry-level employees are graciously tolerated. Most veteran workers do not see new employees as competition and therefore exhibit an air of friendliness and openness. Some seasoned personnel even assume an unofficial role of mentor to new employees, which further eases their transition to the work environment.

As the new kids on the block, no assignment is deemed beneath their job level. Work scorned by others seems to follow them around. This is actually a good thing as long as it doesn't last too long. Learning from the ground up is actually the best kind of experience. Some workers never acquire this foundation. Seasoned workers are not permitted such luxury. They are expected to know everything, and this is where problems can arise. When situations come up that assume a certain degree of knowledge, those not possessing this information often resort to the game of wordsmith artistry. This acquired characteristic becomes a familiar tool to those who must pretend. Later on in your career, the grunt-level experience actually supports your confidence level because you know what you're talking about and, more importantly, others know you know.

So it is wise to recognize that certain benefits are associated with being a new employee.

The Outside Savior

In times of corporate duress in which the current management has been exposed as totally out of touch with reality, the board of directors may appoint an outside savior. Never mind that hundreds of equally qualified individuals who are more familiar with the problems and potential solutions may exist within the corporation. This outsider is usually given a lucrative deal in which her income is laced with bonus clauses, allowing her to make more money even if it rains on Christmas.

The most common technique for the savior to employ is to immediately begin consolidating, reorganizing, and refocusing on the core company businesses, and—shazam—she most likely will determine that the solution is to get rid of lots of employees. Therefore, she may reason, even if revenues remain flat for the foreseeable future, Company X will seem to be on the right track with an improved earnings record. But beware: To have the same improvement the next year, further firings may become the accepted way of enhancing the bottom line. This technique is a surefire winner among saviors who have bestowed their presence on a variety of companies. Such sobriquets as Chainsaw Charlie, Susie the Slasher, and Downsize Dudley often become coveted titles to those who are only interested in making money at all costs. The remaining workers of such cleansed companies often experience longer work hours to make up for the people who were dismissed. After all, these former workers were doing something, not just sitting around discussing Monday night football.

This catharsis works for companies that manufacture manhole covers to companies that are on the leading-edge in aerospace. This increase in profits and decrease in costs usually buys the outside savior time in her battle to raise the stock price (and coincidentally her own income with the stock options granted in her contract). Another favorite technique that some saviors employ to enhance their monetary reward packages is to convince the board of directors to buy back company stock on the open market to give the illusion of financial health. This almost always causes the stock price to rise. Alas, this clever move also increases the value of the stock options granted to the savior. Everybody seems to gain by this action—except that the budget for research and development may be reduced to pay for this artificial stock activity. The future of the company becomes more risky, but then the savior's perspective is never long term. She probably figures she will make her bundle and then move on to the next savior opportunity, citing her record of proven performance.

Although the outside savior does not have to dream up the future strategy of the company, she does have to hold her ego in check long enough to listen to those individuals who can provide the direction. She must be able to recognize which of her advisors she trusts with such a mission. She may play everyone against each other hoping that, with enough scrutiny, a winner will emerge without requiring a decision on her part. It seems that executive decisions are increasingly made by merely delaying any action on the executive's part. Someone else lower in the management chain makes this subconscious move. Remember, managers are, by nature, survivors, and being identified with a losing direction would mean career disaster.

The Sinking Ship

Ever work in an environment in which everyone knows that the products you are helping to develop will be axed? The terminology for such a pending demise is that product development will be stabilized or placed in abeyance. Seasoned employees have come to recognize that stabilization is an accepted euphemism associated with stuff that is not going anywhere. When stabilization gains momentum, it usually leads to the next stage, which is called balancing resources. This occurs when sister departments begin pirating workers and when the company says this work redistribution is a temporary measure needed to "meet current commitments." From this statement, average employees should realize that their projects are probably not considered current but now a distant dream in the eyes of management. Meeting current commitments means that the project is behind schedule and long hours are required to put it back on schedule.

Smart individuals should use this time to actively search for their next jobs because experience shows that their former positions will probably disappear in the meantime. At first, other opportunities are only whispered about in the hallways and other places outside the ear of management. This phase is then followed by confidential phone calls with prospective employers, absences from work, and a dress mode that makes its wearer stand out among other employees. This mode of dress has become known as the interview suit. As more individuals come to grips with their situation and the numbers of nattily attired fellow employees increase, discussions about other job opportunities usually become more open. Comparisons regarding salaries, locations, challenges, and side benefits may monopolize spare moments in the workday. At this point real workers are not afraid that management might hear their conversations because they are resigned to securing employment elsewhere anyway. After the initial individuals leave, morale and productivity may sink to new lows. Others are usually quick to follow, lest they have to stay behind and endure the stigma of remaining with a sinking ship. In these times employees need not feel any remorse about leaving to pursue better opportunities.

Tips for Job Progression and Evaluation

For most people, jobs provide financial resources to enjoy a favorable lifestyle outside the work environment. Other people work to gain power, to gain prestige, and to perform work for work's sake. In the majority of cases, the monetary needs of workers seem to grow with time in order to reach some desired lifestyle goal. Therefore, it is extremely important to have some kind of a plan to take advantage of opportunities that result in employment positions, which build toward an objective. Having such a strategy will force individuals to think about their employment in a different light. A blueprint for career advancement defines goals such as desired compensation level, positions to be attained, and experience to be gained. All these variables are mapped on some time scale. Be realistic to avoid disappointment. Plans can change drastically, and it is OK to change them. They can also accelerate alongside your desire, ability, and recognition of when to get another job.

Positions that have become routine offer little or no opportunity to acquire the experience that comes with new challenges and the accompanying rewards. You cannot grow doing the same things over and over. Be alert to recognize symptoms of non-growth, disparity, and ultimate stagnation. They include the following:

- ✦ A position that is not making good use of skills the you possess. Lack of use decreases your marketability.
- ✦ A position in which you are not learning new skills. Remember that skill mix is better than specialization in the long run. More opportunities simply come your way. Two years' experience two times over doesn't do you any good. Some people have the equivalent of two years' experience and stretch it out for twenty years. In big corporations people can and do hide. Variety of perspective comes with a diverse background.

    ↪ A position that is not involved in the main activities of the company. For example, these can be service- or support-oriented as opposed to positions in product marketing.

    ↪ A position in which the monetary compensation grids[1] for your job classification are below the pay grids for other job classifications in the company. This disparity says that the company does not value your services as much as it does other employees' contributions. It just doesn't matter if your skills are greater, your educational level is superior, or your dedication is more unwavering. The company has decreed that your job is less important.

    ↪ A position with a high turnover rate. The defection of prior employees provides a sound indication of some dissatisfaction.

Don't drift because you have reached a level of comfort. Get a plan. Don't depend on the company's career development plan, for it may benefit not you but the company. Realistically appraise how your present job fits into your career goals.

Company Loyalty and Its Demise

Company loyalty is the tacit agreement between a company and its employees that binds both parties together in the pursuit of complementing benefits. In the case of a business organization, the rewards are profit, customer satisfaction, and opportunity. It is to the company's advantage to foster the notion of loyalty because doing so reduces turnover and the attendant problems associated with a work force retained and motivated only by money. Employees also gain because of the secure employment and other perks offered by such a relationship. All is well until the company enters a phase of financial strain. Then the company may begin to violate this agreement by reducing and/or eliminating company benefits associated with loyalty. In an effort to reduce its cost structure, the company may begin to induce its higher paid workers (the overwhelming

---

[1]Pay grids provide ranges and guidelines for salary compensation/raises that a company specifies for various levels of job performance (adequate, meets requirements, superior, excellent, . . .). The achievement level is associated with various job classifications (engineer, marketer, . . .) and rank within a classification (e.g., trainee, associate, staff, senior, . . .). In big companies, such a structure is a way of controlling costs and creating some degree of uniformity. However, remember that everything is negotiable and there are exceptions for everything.

majority are senior employees, many eligible to retire) to leave. It may decree disincentives to remain employed. Here are a few examples of disincentives:

- Gradually shifting the cost of medical benefits from the company to the employee. The amount of the employee's share increases periodically. So the longer employees elect to remain employed at the company, the greater their retirement medical costs burden becomes.
- Changing the retirement plan by gradually shifting its cost from the company to the employee.
- Announcing that employees now have an opportunity to share in the profits of the company because part of their compensation will be paid based on how well the company profit picture is. Funny thing about this: When profits were huge, employees were never offered this opportunity. Now that profits are low, this variable pay is (in reality) zero for several years. In effect, the company has implemented an across-the-board pay freeze while touting it as a new benefit.
- Effectively disbanding the association of workers who have achieved twenty-five years' employment with the company. This association had activities that were either subsidized or entirely paid for by the company.
- Reducing the cost of its service awards by eliminating expensive options for commemoratives.

After enacting one or more of these disincentives, suddenly the company may discover that workers will retaliate. Employees who formerly worked untold hours of non-compensated overtime may begin to work only forty hours per week. The number of employees from all age brackets who are seeking other employment opportunities may dramatically increase. Even the contractors may leave (an extremely unhealthy sign) because, although they are temporary workers, they can't stand the work environment. No longer do workers go the extra mile because they feel the company has forgotten them. Ironically the company may interpret these defections as a good thing. New management that has no feeling for the culture that made the company prosper may be brought in from outside. After all, new blood and young ideas are touted as a sign of vigor, a sign of the new order. The downside for the company is that the savvy, experience, and dedication are no longer present in its work force. But not to worry—everyone else is doing it too.

Ramifications of the Corporate Direction

Whenever new products and services are needed to maintain the growth of an organization, an official corporate direction is usually announced. The proponents of the strategy must be excellent pitchmen, and they must travel to various locations selling the company's officially sanctioned direction like it was candy. This is not as difficult as it may seem because the big boys need a vision of the future to lead the company into the next decade of profitability. If a strategy void exists, then the management in power is often willing to grab at most anything that tells a good story. Experience teaches that over time most any strategy has a way of evolving into something reasonable . However, in some instances this is not the case.

For example, if employees hear the official corporate direction and decide it is nonsense, then their consciences often coerce dissenting opinions. When these dissenting convictions run counter to what is accepted as the official corporate strategy, then life can become difficult. You may have been a respected member of the company's technical community, but now management may not be willing to tolerate your beliefs. You may be accused of being not part of the team, of becoming a rabble-rouser, or maybe even becoming someone who cannot see progress. Even though your assignment may encompass the new strategy, you may find yourself uninvited to informational meetings. You may even be removed from the distribution list of strategy document recipients. This state of limbo can last for one or even several years.

Over time, other employees may join you in criticizing the strategy. Therefore, when the executives begin to see the strategy's flaws, they must be careful; a "managed evolution" into a totally different corporate direction would be too transparent. Already too many statements of "I told you so" and "what a waste of effort" echo in the hallways. The credibility of management must be maintained, so a neutralized admission of error somehow needs to be made. How might management handle this situation? Two classic maneuvers have been known to be used:

1. Management can say, "Market conditions have changed, thus requiring a change in strategy." This is the most frequent method used to justify such a transformation. The following variations also warrant mentioning:
   - ↪ "Customer task forces indicate that the proposed new products and services are too advanced for their needs."

◆ "Competition dictates that the corporation must focus on current products and services to maintain the company's image of being responsive to its customers' needs."

◆ "The strategy was a super idea, but its costs were prohibitive."

2. When the responsible managers realize the strategy is a failure, they can turn this event to their advantage. They can contrive success in the face of disaster by appearing to be heroes. How? Simple. They can use the technique of "falling on one's sword." This means that failing managers confess their guilt to senior executives before the disaster becomes widely recognized. Consequently, other employees believe that the managers have thus borne the brunt of the failure. The managers' integrity usually increases throughout the company. Neat trick if they can pull it off.

The Importance of a Front Man

By their nature, corporations working on complicated projects have a number of employees who continually monitor the progress of these undertakings. Their main function is to alert other interrelated and/or dependent departments whenever certain objectives might be compromised. These objectives can include a project's schedules, quality, function, and so on. Sometimes conflicting, rumored, and negative information becomes available to these trackers because of a naive management staff that is too busy or inexperienced to appreciate the importance of a good press. Any unflattering news relating to the project can be used to the advantage of other departments (both cooperating and competing) as those departments see fit. For example, such news may offer them the opportunity to slip their schedules, increase their head counts to accommodate a rumored increase in function, or replace the failing product with an alternative. Enter the indispensable front man.

This individual's responsibility is to buffer his boss's department(s) from the outside interference that accompanies almost all product development cycles and in essence prevent and quell any negative information about the project. Above all, he maintains a positive outlook even under the grimmest of circumstances. Usually, he reports to the functional manager in charge. The front man should have an exuberant personality plus an in-depth understanding of the workings of the particular project. He makes it a point to anticipate problems before they occur and gives the appearance of complete openness. Whenever the opportunity to present the status of his boss's project occurs, this individual is more than willing to describe any of its facets. He is an expert chart-maker by necessity. He must give the appearance of cooperation and honesty even though reality might suggest otherwise.

Actually, this employee saves the company both time and money because his functional manager doesn't have to spend valuable resources defending the project once negative vibes begin to surface. Interestingly, most projects undergo periods of great difficulty. However, an experienced management staff will regard this characteristic as normal. Uninitiated managers can add to the bad press when things don't go according to plan. Thus the need for a respected, savvy front man has become accepted corporate practice. As this aspect of corporate life has become more recognized, large corporations have elevated the duties of the front man to (what else) a department of front men.

The Employee Who Hides

Employees who experience heavy workloads for several years often receive assignments that are minimally taxing as a sort of unofficial reward. This tactic is meant to give the employee a rest from past efforts while maintaining the semblance that she is doing productive work. Now, there is nothing unfair about this maneuver when an employee has earned such a rest. However, once it becomes known that such jobs exist, a plethora of candidates surface.

Now it is quite rational to ask, "How do vacation-type jobs come into existence in the first place?" Several methods are worth describing:

- ↬ Management can justify the existence of such departments because a rival function at another corporate site has a similar organization. The multi-location vacation groups then interact, thus contributing to the growth and perpetuation of such activities. Note that once any structure gains a foothold, it becomes difficult to change. It may take years to recognize the uselessness of company-sponsored sabbatical functions.
- ↬ Under the guise of advancement (in planning, technology, design, architecture, finance, or whatever), these employment descriptions all begin with good intentions. Who can argue that a real need to do something for the future exists? However, what usually occurs is a lengthy wordsmith game among people who have no real responsibility to produce anything. When it comes time to actually

do something, they usually turn that responsibility over to other departments. Interestingly, the individuals who work in the "advanced" department hardly ever transfer to a doer capacity. Somehow, the word *advanced* contributes to their elevated opinions of their abilities, and those opinions can last for a long time.

↪ Some employees were given holding-pattern jobs when their functions were discontinued. These jobs were only meant to exist until productive work surfaced. However, the nature of those involved in the management game is to expand anything under their influence, whatever that may be. After all, a large portion of managers' own advancement depends on pyramid structures.

Several unfavorable things can happen to an employee while functioning in leisure mode. First, her job skills can become obsolete during an extended rest period. In a fast-moving technology corporation, this time period can be quite brief. If she is young, this could be mentally disastrous. However, if she is in the latter part of her career, the effect becomes less important. So, over time, career rest-stops tend to be populated by senior workers. This is unfortunate because many of these people were star performers when they were in a doer capacity. Second, her job habits may begin to deteriorate. Coming to work late, taking extended lunch breaks, increasing the number of coffee chats, and obsessing with the accumulation of frequent flier miles, all can contribute to her performance decline.

Although it is possible to hide out for years in company-sponsored furloughs, remember that you, the individual employee, are responsible for your own career destiny.

Professional Contract Workers

Companies like to employ people on a temporary basis to perform duties normally done by a company's own workers. Companies do this because they can save money by not giving these workers benefits, such as pension or health; because these temporary employees may possess skills not available within the organization; and because the employment of these workers can be terminated at any time. These individuals, called contractors, are usually employed for fixed periods of time, such as a year. They work alongside the company's regular employees. How do the regular employees react to this? Let's take a look at what can happen.

Much to their dismay, the company's regular employees may soon discover the pay differential favors the contractors by a large percentage (sometimes a three-digit percentage). Not only may the contractors' regular forty-hour wages be significantly higher than those of company workers performing the same job, but the contractors usually get paid for working overtime too. They often earn time and a half for time that exceeds forty hours per week and maybe even double time for working on Sunday. Meanwhile, the company may try to appease its regular workers by reminding them that the contractors are not receiving any company benefits. In fact, they may be receiving these benefits directly from the contracting company, or if this is not the case, they can pay for them out-of-pocket because of the significant amount of their paycheck differentials. Does this affect employee morale? Sure it does. Is the company concerned that morale is negatively affected? You can answer this question yourself by checking to see whether or not the contractors remain employed after the morale problem is acknowledged. Does the company really save money by hiring contract workers? For the long run, the answer is "no" or "not clear" at best.

A contractor who is hired because he possesses a highly sought skill may or may not prove capable of performing that skill. Remember that one reason people choose to work as contractors is to gain experience in a certain area while getting paid to do it. So instead of the company getting the benefit of a trained worker, sometimes the contractor benefits in this kind of relationship. Then the contractor takes his newly acquired skills with him when his term of employment expires.

In the everyday work environment, these temporary workers are not really part of the company, so their attendance at meetings that are political in nature is prohibited. The pleasant side effect of this condition is they can devote more time to performing the work they were hired to do. Therefore companies often perceive contractors as more productive simply because they are not involved in required activities that affect regular employees.

The effect of this employment shift to contract workers will result in a work force that changes jobs frequently with no feelings of company loyalty. Company pensions will be supplemented and/or replaced by contributions to a retirement plan that employees can take with them from job to job. Employees need to regard their own employment as being in business for themselves.

Tactics Workers Use to Irritate Management

Whenever workers and management are at odds, workers use a number of maneuvers to vent their displeasure. It is best if these happenings occur within the boundaries of remaining good employees, but this is not always the case. For example, when an employee does not trust her manager, she may begin to document all the events that show her in a favorable light while recording selected manager's activities, which are mostly negative. (Note that this particular tactic can work both ways because this is often the main strategy managers use to build a case against an employee they wish to reprimand or fire.) Trivial things have a way of building up to a state of great importance.

Some irritation tactics that have been known to occur include the following:

- Substituting written communication for items that were previously handled verbally
- Walking out of a meeting when the eight-hour day is done, even though the meeting is still in session
- Openly discussing a manager's shortcomings with co-workers
- Not supporting one's manager in a meeting, even though the manager solicited that person's backing
- Questioning every management directive—even those with indisputable validity
- Advertising one's accomplishments to an excess
- Using formal language in conversation with one's manager, even though this complicates the communication, or using buzzwords and phrases that are unfamiliar to one's manager
- Turning up one's frequency of complaints concerning the cafeteria food, the limited number of restrooms, distant parking facilities, and so on
- Formally requesting a meeting with one's manager through the secretary rather than informally talking to him when he has some free time
- Not copying one's manager on important correspondence

The previously mentioned confrontation strategies surely can negatively affect productivity. When these signals are recognized, management should initiate a frank discussion with the employee. Unfortunately, the offended manager sometimes retaliates, often producing a full-scale personality conflict. This should be avoided at all costs, as this game will become all too obvious to those watching from the sideline. It becomes infectious, and everyone loses.

The Illusion of Advancement Through Job Transfer

Management likes to groom employees for eventual positions of power and responsibility—especially future management positions. To gain experience rapidly, employees who must be groomed are usually given a variety of tasks to expose them to the inner workings of a large corporation. Such assignments are usually of short duration, so often a groomee really never has a chance to accomplish anything significant. Therefore, these selected individuals cannot fail because they won't have time to do anything wrong. After years and years of grooming, these people re-enter the ranks of the gainfully employed. Now they must finally do something without having done real work for awhile. Companies refer to people so chosen as "on the fast track." Beware of such people because they have cultivated important friends who have a vested interest in their careers.

What happens to individuals who are not on the fast track but who want to remain employed by the same company? One convenience that only a big company can afford is creating the illusion of success via the employee-initiated transfer. However, if this is not in the interest of the local management, a petition for such a transfer can be stalled for years and years.

The prudent employee understands how this game is played. First, it is unwise to place your request in the transfer pool, hoping someone will offer you a job. Most often these available jobs are not oriented to any career goals you might have. They are usually oriented toward a lot of hard work that the current staff can't or won't do. So what do aspiring non-fast-track employees usually do? First they poll their network of company allies and find out about openings that suit their career goals. Next they convince the receiving locations to ask their current managers if they are available for opportunities in other organizations. In this way, it appears they are not involved, and so they retain the appearance of loyalty. Then their prospective managers must build cases to show these transfers would be in the best interests of the company. If the new position involves a physical move to another city, the perception of advancement is guaranteed. When an employee transfers to corporate headquarters, this perception assumes even more credibility.

People have also been known to use the employee-initiated transfer to accomplish other objectives, such as living in a warmer climate, obtaining a pay raise, jumping ship to avoid a disaster, broadening their experience, and so on. This tactic can be used multiple times during an employee's career with no apparent ill effects. Besides, management wants employees who have not limited their work experiences to one or two specialties.

How to Recognize a Good Job

A good job today might not be·a good job tomorrow. Industries, companies, and jobs change over time. The only sure bet is that change is for certain, and education is the best way to prepare for any transition. So be flexible in your expectations, and don't just stay in a job because it provides a level of comfort, security, status, and income. All things are subject to change. Periodically evaluate the opportunities afforded outside your present employer, and be prepared to move. Avoid surprises.

Assuming that an individual's current responsibilities allow the freedom to move on, the best time to consider an employment move is when an available position's duties and responsibilities are relatively undefined. Don't let lack of stability deter you from taking a chance. The newness of the job's requirements indicates challenge, risk, and the potential to "get in on the ground floor." In effect, you get to participate in the evolution of the job.

This job may open up in a brand-new company or even be in an established corporation that has developed something whose ramifications are not well understood. The Human Resources (HR) Department must support the unknowns of a job whose requirements are new and not defined. It does this by hiring individuals who possess various academic disciplines and experience. HR hopes that this trial-and-error hiring practice eventually develops into a profile that indicates the best chance for success in the workplace. HR may even add to the position's mystique by utilizing tests to determine a person's inclinations and aptitude. Much time can elapse before academia comes to the rescue by defining new courses and maybe even new disciplines to satisfy requirements for these new-fashioned jobs.

In the early stages of this new-job era, most applicants tend to be recent graduates because older, experienced workers are inclined to take fewer chances. As a result, the population of these new-type jobs mainly consists of people at the beginnings of their careers. This characteristic contributes to a certain comradeship, which fosters other benefits, like good communication and low employee turnover. This euphoria may last for several years until the job and people mature. Remember that things change and management may now view this free and easy atmosphere as undesirable. Management may eventually dictate that the new-job era needs more structure, more discipline, and more accountability—an indication of pending bureaucracy. When this happens, the new-job era turns into a more traditional type of job.

For positions requiring traditional technical skills, like engineering and programming, the ground-floor opportunity occurs when a new project is being staffed. This is when the most learning occurs. This is when the "experts" are born. In this situation, you get to see the big picture of both the *why* and the *how*. Your chances for meaningful contributions increase. Your notoriety is also enhanced. People who hire on later rarely have the opportunity to gain the same perspective.

A Job Misrepresented

Occasionally, employees find themselves doing jobs that are represented as a challenge but in reality involve drudgery, uncompensated overtime, and even a misuse of their talents. Sometimes companies rely on specious phrases to secure an individual's acceptance for such unpleasantness. Statements such as "Business conditions have changed," "You are needed to support a critical deadline," "The experience will broaden your skills," "This project has the attention of upper management," "You need to get more involved," and "This assignment is temporary," all can place your career on temporary hold or even in jeopardy. The following unexpected repercussions of a job misrepresented can also work against you later:

- A periodic performance evaluation may reveal that you have been working at a skill level rated beneath your job classification. In other words you are being paid too much money based on the level of work you are doing. Your ranking will likely fall, and you then will run the risk of a demotion. This can occur even if you agreed to the assignment for the benefit of the company.
- While you busily try to meet the commitments made by others, career-enhancing assignments that become available during that time may pass you by.
- Job reassignments have long been used to remove an employee who is not compatible with the manager's personality. As you might suspect, there may be nothing temporary about your job change.
- Your current talents can become rusty or outdated. It will be increasingly difficult to extricate yourself from exile the longer you remain in a disagreeable situation.
- The unpleasant assignment may require skills you do not currently possess. It is not irrational to suspect that this temporary deficiency can be used to lower your performance ranking.

⤙ Perhaps your contrary viewpoint on a highly debated project prompted a management-directed exile into oblivion. Because you have been removed from these contested discussions, your reputation may suffer because your perspective is never defended. It may even become the object of ridicule.

Be careful of any consequences associated with accepting a new job assignment. Verbal assurances from your manager may evaporate. You may never return to work for your current boss, and then all bets will be off. Take time to appreciate this impact on your career objectives. Document your concerns as a condition of accepting any management-suggested job change. Make sure these concerns are kept in your personnel jacket. This defensive tactic is well worth the effort, if just to let management know you will not be unknowingly manipulated.

If these job reassignment tactics occur frequently, then it is time to look for another job outside the company. At this point, you may safely assume the company views your talents as commodities rather than valued skills. Your present employer is also limiting your opportunities because you never stay in one job long enough to acquire the recognition required for promotion. Look out for yourself by moving on.

The Sit-in Manager Experience

An absence from work by a member of the management team offers an opportunity for individuals aspiring entry into the field of supervision. In a way that is similar to the workings of the military, a substitute individual is usually chosen to represent the views of an administrator who will not be physically present in the workplace for some period of time. This activity may be surrounded with a lot of formality. Notes may be sent to members of the department and peer managers within the organization, and these notes usually contain phrases like, "Joe Ambitious will handle personnel concerns during my absence, and Wendy Work-A-Lot will handle technical affairs." Much of the time, employees may not notice that their manager is missing from work, so they often greet such announcements as unneeded administrivia.

The most obvious occurrence that happens on the first day of a sit-in's tenure is he occupies the office of his manager. This action usually gives the surrogate a taste of power. It is important that he maintains the perception that everything is running smoothly. An absent manager will often instruct the replacement to do nothing, for fear he might make a commitment outside the department. In fact, this may be the first time the sit-in manager has had to appear busy when there was nothing to do.

The sit-in's simulated work activities may include talking on the phone, attending meetings, answering queries with innocuous replies so as not to make a mistake, reading periodicals, telling upper management that everything is on schedule, and talking to the secretary. Whenever the absent manager returns to work, the surrogate may divulge that he really didn't do anything. The manager will probably take this commentary as an endorsement of how well the department is being managed.

The Company As a Commodity

Once, turnover was looked upon as a bad thing. However, today's enlightened-worker attitudes welcome it. Corporations, just like employees, have become commodities, and employees should not hesitate to trade up once in a while.

The employee benefits situation provides a clear reason why companies should be treated as commodities. The costs of employee benefits are increasingly shifting from corporations to their employees. This change includes both medical and retirement expenses. Let's look at how this pertains to employee retirement. Let's say Jill Employee must put money away for her retirement through a new savings plan controlled by the company. Her company now even contributes some monetary percentage to this new savings plan, boosting the perception that the old retirement plan is being phased out in favor of one that is improved. (Actually, the company saves money this way.) But wait—companies didn't really analyze the consequences of this strategy. The corporation is expunging the very program that persuaded its workers to remain in a long-term employment commitment. Of utmost importance is that Jill Employee now gets to take this savings-plan money with her when she secures a better position elsewhere. In times past, workers lost every cent they had accrued when they changed companies unless a required number of employment years had been met. But now Jill Employee can simply transfer this money to the plan sponsored by her new employer or even to a private retirement (tax-wise choice) account. As far as health plans are concerned, the advent of "managed care" neutralized most advantages a company had in gaining any loyalty-inducement advantage over its competitors. So benefits as a differentiator among companies are disappearing. The focus on the employee's salary or other forms of current income has become the main corporate differential. The move to another company is becoming more and more palatable.

Another reason employees should change companies every so often involves job skills. One of the most frequently stated management critiques of professional employees is that their job skills or experience needs broadening. They are often told that education and training to obtain additional capabilities are the employee's responsibility. Individuals are sometimes even passed over for promotion because of their lack of varied experience. The easiest way to expand your background is to get a new job periodically, just to add to your experience portfolio. Don't fear that you may lack the necessary skills. You will, in effect, learn by doing. It's the best avenue for retentive knowledge. It is common knowledge in large corporations that specialization is not good for a person's career. Therefore work to become a generalist because the variety of your acquired skills (including verbal acuity to enhance perceived worth) is more prized than ever. So when a company urges employees to expand their skills and experience, the company does not fully realize the consequences of this action. The individuals become more marketable commodities both inside and outside their present employer. Bouncing around from company to company has become acceptable in today's work force, and it is actually good for a career. By doing so, in mid-career a person's resume looks much more impressive when compared with the resume of an individual whose experience is limited to a single corporation.

The time to start looking for a new job begins on the first day of employment at any company. The search can include opportunities both inside and outside your present employer. Never quit your present job out of frustration before you have another job lined up because it is far easier to get a job if you already have one. Let's look at a few of the positives of this statement:

- If you already have a job, there is less time pressure to find another because you are still receiving a paycheck from your current employer.
- By being employed, your network of contacts remains current.
- Your bargaining power is enhanced when a potential employer believes it has to entice you to leave your present position.
- You get a realistic evaluation of your marketability. Negative prospects may convince a job opportunist to stay put.

Employees should shed corporations just like corporations shed people. People have come to learn that a secure position in a large company is an anachronism in today's business climate.

How Some People Communicate Without Revealing Their Lack of Understanding

Some people in the workplace have decided it is always better to appear in the know than to admit they may not be acquainted with a particular subject. These people have learned they instead can solicit an educational response without revealing their lack of understanding. They think it makes them look better to say, "What's your opinion on Topic X?" than to say, "I don't understand Topic X." This is especially true if they are supposed to know about a particular subject. Managers, marketing people, planners, lawyers, and others who make their living by talking often have highly developed skills in this regard. Many new employees learn this aspect of the work environment quickly. It gives them a feeling of belonging when they use phrases like "We need to understand the customer's needs" and "Exactly what are the requirements?" Admittedly, failure to incorporate "in" words and phrases can give others the view that you are just not keeping up with the job requirements. In contrast, the perception that you are savvy is continually reinforced whenever you appear to be in the know. Some people accomplish this by using phrases such as the following:

- ✎ "I think you have legal problems."
- ✎ "What does marketing think?"
- ✎ "What does the competition offer?"
- ✎ "The product ship date looks too optimistic."
- ✎ "Describe the performance limitations."

Notice that these phrases are product independent. The person who says them does not have to have the faintest idea about the topic on the table. All these phrases solicit a response that will teach that person more about what is being discussed without the individual appearing completely baffled. Then the person can absorb what was said and use that knowledge to further his or her understanding of the topic under debate. However, people who employ this method should be careful not to re-use these particular words/phrases in subsequent meetings too soon. Their tactics would then become too obvious, especially to others who use the same technique. The thing to learn here is that by becoming accustomed to using such language, some people appear to understand everything. They may even find themselves inventing other global words/phrases that apply to almost any situation. Their reputations continue to be enhanced.

How a Manager Can Ease Out a Competent Worker

A number of reasons can cause a manager to try to get rid of employees, even when they perform adequately. Some of the more noteworthy motivations are as follows:

- ✧ An employee has not shown the proper respect to a manager and thus offends his ego.
- ✧ An employee tells it like it is rather than saying what the manager wants to hear. Some individuals just don't like to hear about problems.
- ✧ A manager sees her employee as a competitor. In cases such as this, a manager usually doesn't manage because she still wants to do the technical work.
- ✧ An employee is identified as not being a team player. The definition of *team* is somewhat subjective in the context of a managed department. It's difficult to prove that you are indeed a team player when this charge is leveled at you.
- ✧ The employee's personal habits (such as working late, dressing too casually, and not playing the overtime game) differ from those of the manager.

Corporations have discovered that it is not difficult to terminate employees in cases of job incompetence. In fact a management procedure called the measured mile is in place to implement this facet. The measured-mile process says that an individual is given a certain task to perform during some limited time frame. If the task is not satisfactorily completed, then the company may fire the employee. Unfortunately, this technique can be indiscriminately used to get rid of good employees (even superstars) when the real reason is akin to the points previously mentioned. Sometimes managers use this corporate-sanctioned technique to suit their own needs. Unfortunately, this includes dealing with personnel problems, both real and imagined.

One noteworthy example of this abuse involves an excellent employee who happened to tell his manager what he thought about the company's visionary project and all the company verbosity that surrounded it. The manager took this defilement personally and decided to get rid of him. So the manager resorted to using the measured mile. The assignment involved assessing some facet of a rather large interdivisional project that the corporation had been wrestling with for several years. There were no easy answers, and everyone knew it. The measured employee worked overtime on his assignment because he knew he could be fired for failing to comply. Everyone else knew the real reason why the employee was put on the measured mile: Joe Manager's ego was bruised. The net result of Joe's actions was to lose the respect of the other workers, for they knew the affronting employee to be an excellent performer.

The Dodge-and-Weave Show

The notion of open communication is sometimes fostered by a management staff that has another agenda to accomplish. Take the case of regularly scheduled meetings (for example, biweekly) that everyone is invited to attend for the purpose of listening to a top-level manager discuss everything and anything. These meetings may get high visibility in order to demonstrate management's commitment to keep everyone updated on the latest happenings. Now if the company was doing great (financially, technically, or otherwise), these meetings would probably never happen. The unspoken management goal here may be to appease a worker staff that needs assurance that things are not as bad as they seem—to make it appear that management has everything under control. Sometimes the company publicizes that any question will be answered but that employees must submit them in advance so management can adequately address the questions. This should be Clue No. 1 that things may not be completely aboveboard. So such a gathering commences, and the dodge-and-weave show begins.

First, to relax audience members and perhaps disarm their hostility, the speaker may enthusiastically tell about a series of humorous scenarios regarding her exploits in a customer office. Now, experienced employees may know that most of the described antics would not be tolerated by any consumer. However, this does not stop such a gifted rhetorician. People laugh, and the speaker gains confidence that she is succeeding in manipulating the audience's way of thinking. Next she needs to enhance the perception that she is an important executive (and therefore highly compensated). She may do this by telling a story about buying jewelry, not from a store but from a representative invited into her home for a personal showing. She may tell about how she told the jewelry salesperson that, as an important executive of her company, she can't waste time by shopping as others who are less moneyed do. The audience now may be really impressed because this highly paid individual has taken time out of her busy schedule to speak to the troops. This tactic is usually effective because the speaker has established her credentials not by saying anything important but by associating herself with money and power. Such maneuvers set the stage for the real reason people have come to hear Jane Executive speak.

The question-and-answer session begins. However, without the employees realizing it, the speaker has already managed to waste a large part of the meeting discussing subjects of her own choosing. The time allotted to address the real purpose of such a gathering is nearing an end. Nevertheless, *selected* employee questions that were presubmitted are discussed with some degree of credibility, and things appear to be going well. However, the hard questions never seem to surface. Suddenly the meeting is almost over, and the savvy employee correctly assumes that his question will never be discussed. So he asks the speaker the query aloud. The presenter continues to extend the illusion that she has everything under control and may attempt to disarm the verbal bullet with a bit of deprecation. She may respond to the inquiry by saying, "You don't understand" or better yet, "You missed the point." The audience now probably thinks that such a question is stupid because the esteemed speaker has said so.

If this happens to you, be persistent. Re-state your question in simpler terms. The audience will listen closely for a reply. Jane Executive then probably will give an answer that has absolutely nothing to do with the question. She may then sense that the audience now has some doubt about her intentions. It is time to answer your own question. Tell the speaker why your answer is correct. The dodge-and-weave show likely will then move into high gear. The speaker may re-word your answer to present it in a light more favorable to management's way of thinking. Sensing that all is not well, the speaker may diffuse the confusion and attendant tension by saying, "The question will be discussed outside the meeting because time has expired." This may satisfy most, but such a meeting will probably never occur. Your inner self will say, "Write this person off."

Shifts in Company Behavior

Company-sponsored events executed with taste generally promote goodwill between management and workers. In the past, family-oriented happenings in particular tended to renew the employee's sense of loyalty coveted by successful corporations. However, this faithfulness seems to have lost its value to organizations that have begun to treat their staff as a kind of commodity. In many companies today, short-lived entertainment incidents have replaced these family events. This is perfectly acceptable and appropriate in companies with work forces composed of mostly young workers. However, mature enterprises often think that they too must engage in such tactics, possibly because they are in the same business sector as some of their upstart competitors. In the process they often alienate experienced workers who felt more in tune with the family gatherings. Some examples of the new entertainment events include the following:

- Happy hours at which the company pays for the beverages
- Fully clothed pool-jumping adventures by management
- Bungee-jumping escapades by members of management
- Rock band concerts

Rather than rely on what made their companies successful in the first place, corporations often panic when they see other companies trying new things, and so they change for the sake of change.

The Support Group Marvels

Corporations often rely on a favorite expression to deflect criticism regarding the manageability of such a large enterprise. Whenever doubt exists about an organization's ability to weed out ill-conceived ventures, runaway project costs/schedules, or whatever, many companies invoke the phrase "checks and balances" to calm any doubting Thomas. This phrase means that the company has watchdog departments, processes, and techniques that monitor, follow, evaluate, extrapolate, escalate, and ensure that the wayward stuff doesn't happen for long. Sounds great. But let's take a closer look.

The implementation of such safeguards results in built-in mechanisms that slow things down considerably. What may happen is that corporate functions—like product development and manufacturing—subconsciously slant their work efforts to pass inspection of these support group watchdogs. This, of course, detracts from the main focus of any company, which is to bring in revenue and satisfy its customers. Unforeseen is the gradual realization that support activities begin to take precedence over producing functions. Yet the company continually relies on these adjunct services as necessary to avoid making any snafu. Mistakes can be avoided, but this occurs at the expense of time, money and market share.

Without admitting it, the large company has provided another career path for the ambitious employee—the support group career path. This secondary employment option can soon develop into a multi-layered structure rivaling its monitored sibling departments. (Note that a lot of job descriptions that exist in big corporations have no counterparts in smaller competitor companies.) The corporate bureaucracy enjoys an increase in numbers thanks to the support group benefactor.

Unfortunately, doing tangible things can easily become less rewarding than working in the support group. Regular work can be perceived as mundane, routine, or boring. Conversely, monitoring and evaluating productive activities (with complementary charts and colorful presentations) exposes employees to managers, who sometimes use these support groups as a crutch. It's simply easier for some managers to have support groups pitch information to them than to walk around among the workers and gather their own information. For high-level executives this is forgivable, but even first-line managers sometimes resort to this method to obtain knowledge about their own departments. It should not be too much to expect managers to know more about their own functions than any support group tracking the functions' activities.

Smaller companies often take advantage of this huge-enterprise support-group plague to bring new products to market sooner. Also their costs are less (minimal watchdog expenses). In these companies, forecasting is replaced with real market experience, and many of the corporate games associated with being big simply cannot exist. Percentage-wise, there are far more doers in small companies than in large corporations because people cannot hide for years without doing anything useful. However, an unexpected benefit that big corporations realize from their smaller relatives is they get to monitor the success or failure of their rival's latest products and services. They then can react accordingly. Some large-company proponents of this tactic do not seem to realize that they have reverted to a reactive posture and have left innovation to their more nimble competitors. In the long run, the small company gets bigger and ultimately falls into the same support group trap as its predecessors. The rise and fall of big corporations continues.

Some Interesting Occurrences Preceding a Product's Demise

Whenever a developing project is not well accepted in the corporation, there is usually no lack of individuals who criticize it at every opportunity. These people know they can derive as much notoriety from stopping a project as from supporting a successful one. Some big companies actually reward people who kill projects. Although killing a work effort is viewed as a short-term endeavor, a string of product assassinations can be just as career enhancing as one or two notable successes.

Seldom is a project axed from within. Axing seems to be the domain of exterior groups, which often accomplish the axing in a specious atmosphere of fairness and objectivity. Here is the process they usually use:

- ↬ Symptoms of a product's collapse begin to surface in the form of seemingly harmless inquiries from outside functions. This is the first step in gathering information (evidence) and is used to lend credibility to the killing process. Such information (both real and extrapolated) can be manipulated to achieve the desired result.
- ↬ The product's supporters may then be asked to provide scenarios that show how their effort fits into the corporation's strategic plan. (Everyone knows the corporate plan is generally soft so it can be readily changed to absorb/reflect reality.) Innocuous arguments ensue about what is strategic and what is tactical. This activity often turns into an exercise in verbal acuity but is meant to convey the illusion of thoroughness and importance.
- ↬ The product's detractors then invoke a maneuver meant to give the impression of further impartiality. This tactic is known as the product audit. A series of meetings that investigate the validity of schedules, quality, function, and so on follows. The audit team may even be populated with individuals who suspect the desired results. As expected, the audit usually provides the basis for discontinuing the work effort.

In rare cases the entire process of killing a product can be exercised in reverse and used to the product's supporters' advantage. The end result may be that the product passed close examination and the recommendation is that it be continued. All along, however, this may have been a plan to boost a failing product's credibility. As you can see, appearances can disguise purpose.

Quality Assurance's Role in Large Corporations

Products made for customer delivery are subject to a large degree of testing to validate any claims made by the development departments. These people rightly demand specifications for everything that makes up a product. Endless checkpoints are defined to ensure the product does what it is supposed to do, and the entire process becomes quite formalized. However, some notable abuses of this activity can occur as the game is played:

1. In times of tight product-delivery schedules, rules may be bent, deals made, and products shipped that compromise the integrity of the whole process. Phrases like "The customer wants it now," "We can test it at the customer's location," and "All products have some bugs," sometimes help justify shipping a product before it is ready. However, the bitterness of compromising a product usually lingers long after the sweetness of meeting a schedule, especially for individuals who must deal with customer complaints.

2. When a product is progressing satisfactorily through the testing phase, quality assurance (QA) sometimes abuses its power by doing the following things:
   - Holding up the delivery of products for the slightest reason, even if no customer would ever encounter the flaw.
   - Claiming a large part of the credit for putting out a good product even though QA had no hand in the definition of that product.
   - Panicking corporate management to a degree larger than warranted by the actual crisis to obtain recognition.

Six Sigma: A Mystic Device of Management

Recently a lot of accolades have been bestowed on the mechanisms that aid in producing quality products. Repetitive manufacturing processes have achieved good results with a process known as six sigma. (Bear with me for a moment as I briefly explain it.) The Greek letter sigma is a measure of general variability in statistics, and it is commonly known as the standard deviation. Designated by the symbol σ (the lowercase Greek letter sigma), it is defined as the square root of the average of the squared deviations from the mean. The number six means that the probability of producing a particular widget outside plus or minus multiples of such deviations in a normal curve distribution is extremely unlikely.

This is heavy stuff meant to lend the credibility of statistical mathematics to processes that produce the same things over and over. The term *sigma* has a certain level of abstraction, and management sometimes uses it to surround itself by a cloak of omniscience. Here is what can happen when an organization embraces the six sigma phenomenon. Soon after its introduction, the term *six sigma* usually begins to permeate the corporation. No manager wants to be left off the bandwagon. The cliche "one size fits all" may engulf the thinking of managers so much that they want to apply this new gadget to every possible situation. Suddenly everyone in the corporation may have a six sigma plan for his or her area of responsibility. Meetings may be held expounding the virtues of six sigma. Unfortunately the people making the pitch may be so caught up in the hoopla that they can't answer even the most primitive questions from inquiring employees. Jobs that are not repetitive but require analytical thinking may be suddenly thrust into the jaws of a consuming six sigma blitzkrieg. Employees who write creative architecture and development documents may be told the documents must be six sigma compliant. No one is able to tell them exactly what that means, but the propaganda just won't stop.

The reception of this new tool across the corporation's professional ranks is probably one of absolute skepticism. Words such as *nonsense* and *unbelievable* may echo from the offices of workers engaged in six sigma debates. What does management do to quell the discontent? It may interpret these signs of rebellion as a need for education about six sigma. *Surely there is nothing fundamentally flawed with this latest corporate directive,* managers think. So the ruse continues, and more time is spent in meetings discussing this newly discovered panacea. Examples of cost-saving achievements are touted, but still employees receive no explanation of the applicability of six sigma. Some managers may even begin to recognize the folly in this venture, but no one wants to risk his or her career in defiance of the corporate directive. Guess what—eventually there is less and less talk about this elixir, and six sigma gradually disappears from the scene. Time seems to cure anything.

This discussion shows the following truths:

- First, some managers' willingness to latch onto anything is what appears to make them look good.
- Second, blind obedience is not always prudent. Unfortunately, being a member of the team can cause many managers to lose their objectivity.
- Last, with such an occurrence, the communication gap between the workers and management usually deepens in the areas of trust, credibility, and loyalty.

The Modern Professional

The first thing the modern professional must realize is that a company's concern for its employees usually ends in times of financial duress. All the company tells you about respect for the individual, pay scales that beat the industry average by 10 percent, free medical coverage, liberal pensions, and so on may be quickly dumped in varying degrees to decrease a company's costs. The erosion of benefits is an easy way to bring huge rewards to the company coffers. Unfortunately, it is also a first sign of a company in gradual decline. Ironically, great sums of money and stock options are usually granted to people brought in to oversee this cost-cutting program. Where do the liquid assets come from? Usually from the pockets of the workers. Corporations may defend this action by saying they can no longer afford these expensive benefits. "Times have changed," they may say. So be it. Prepare for the day when this may happen to you. Treat the company as a temporary place of employment to help you gain experience. Remember that loyalty is not a marketable skill; it's a company method to decrease employee turnover during times of plenty.

As a modern professional, the second thing you must learn is to never let yourself get comfortable in the meeting-game antics. Nothing can detract from your effectiveness more than occupying space at a conference table day after day. Don't let anyone tell you that you need to broaden your experience by participating in such meetings. Insist on doing real things that permit you to add to your skill inventory. In the end, you and you alone are responsible for maintaining your marketability. You even get to take these intellectual assets with you when you leave. As a side benefit of doing real work, your true value will finally be recognized when your current employer is under duress. Your work efforts will finally be appreciated. So don't let yourself drift into the trap of game talking and company politics.

Companies that hire experienced people look for accomplishments that demonstrate initiative, skill, creativity, thoroughness, and a discipline to follow through in the face of unforeseen barriers. If you are used to working, then these attributes are easy to accumulate. If you are a game player, then you are somewhat stuck with your present employer. The resumes of game-playing people contain phrases like "monitored product development," "tracked the competition's progress," "participated in strategic planning," and "evaluated" but seldom, "I did. . . ."

It is not only wise to keep your resume updated but also to constantly nurture the network of acquaintances you have accumulated from work, school, previous employers, and so on. These individuals are valuable contacts who come across various opportunities in their everyday activities. Always be on the lookout for a new job, a new location, and more money. Play the game like a corporation does. Charge what the market will bear. Remember that everything is negotiable.

Invariably, it is better to negotiate for a new position when you already have one. You will feel no urgency to accept an offer. Today, having a lengthy employment history with only one or two companies is viewed negatively by potential employers. They believe that by bouncing around to various employers you gain a great deal of valuable experience. This used to be called job hopping, which signified instability and even incompetence. This is no longer the perception. The rules have changed. It is better to think of yourself as a contractor possessing valuable skills. Current trends indicate that most professional jobs—including lawyers, engineers, programmers, accountants, marketers, technical writers, and even managers—will eventually evolve into this model (some already have). Companies will only keep a marginal staff of professional employees to maintain a semblance of an enterprise.

Looking for a New Position

All skilled professional workers should review certain items before testing the employment market. For example, timing can play a significant part in securing a valued position that occasionally surfaces. Therefore, the fact that you are currently employed offers the benefit of an unhurried decision. A leisurely employment search will more likely uncover opportunities that occur infrequently. This is one reason you should always have a current resume ready. You should also conduct a skill inventory to determine the degree of your marketability. You may make the pleasant discovery that you are severely underpaid. This circumstance can happen because your current employer does not appreciate your contributions or falsely assumes that your naivete is sufficient to deter any job change. If your investigation reveals that you are adequately compensated or even overpaid, then perhaps a change in employment is not a wise thing to consider. However, unpleasant working conditions can enhance any justification to move.

A job search officially begins by utilizing methods such as making personal inquiries, networking through acquaintances, or contacting reputable headhunters. Treating this experience like an adventure will remove some of the anxiety associated with meeting new people and evaluating new opportunities. Early in your career, obtaining a variety of experience should be a major objective. Whenever a personal interview results from these activities, however, be prepared for some gamesmanship of another order.

Be inquisitive during any interview. After all, you are risking a temporary career detour, while a large corporate employer is only risking a tryout. If you don't somehow fit into the corporate team, you can easily be replaced. Actually, companies like to advertise that no one is critical to the operation of the big corporation. Gather as many facts about the position as possible. Facts are always better than broad phrases that can be massaged to fit even the most boring assignments. Asking penetrating questions may not endear you to a prospective employer, but this can reduce the chance for disappointment and is preferable to receiving a false impression. Remember that the interview works both ways. Companies don't hire people to reduce the unemployment rate. They employ people because they expect to make a profit on them. Although it is easy to be misled, ask the following types of questions:

1. "Exactly what will be the nature of my initial assignment?" Don't accept a response that goes something like, "The needs of the corporation are still being evaluated." This is a sign that the corporation is simply trying to accumulate bodies.
   - "How long will it last?"
   - "How much (if any) travel is involved?"
   - "What are the schedule commitments?"
   - "What are the functional commitments?"
2. "How much overtime is expected?"
   - "Is it compensated?"
   - "Is there a policy of granting time off during lull periods for uncompensated overtime?"
3. "What is the experience level of others working on the same project?"
   - "Are they new hires?"
4. "How many individuals will I be working with?" This gives some indication of the amount of communication required to accomplish anything. Less is better in most instances.
5. "What are the career possibilities open to me if I accept this job?"
6. "What relocation expenses are reimbursed?"
   - "What limits are there on moving expenses?"
7. "How often are merit raises given?"
8. "What are other benefits I can expect?"

You may not get a satisfactory answer to all these queries, but you need to evaluate the responses just like the company interviewer is evaluating your responses to his or her questions. Above all, don't think any company is doing you a favor by granting an interview. Be polite yet direct.

Failure

Employees fail in their assignments at work for a lot of reasons. Some failures are the fault of the individual; some are the fault of management. The following cases are among the reasons attributed to the individual workers:

- Employees sometimes fail because their personalities do not appropriately meet the demands of their assignments. For example, an excellent engineer may choose to join a marketing organization because of imagined opportunities. Subsequently, the engineer may discover a strong dislike for greeting every problem with a smile and a handshake. Engineers like to meet problems head on. Marketers have to look at the bright side of everything even in the face of a pending disaster.
- Employees sometimes fail because they lack the necessary background (for example, education or training) to handle particular tasks. They may think they can do a job but then discover their skills don't quite satisfy the requirements of the job. This type of personal failure is difficult to admit. However the optimist writes off a failed effort as just another learning experience. Often a worker can acquire the necessary background on the job. In fact, stretching from one job to the next is an accepted way to succeed.
- Employees sometimes fail because of insufficient self-motivation. This may occur when employees accept assignments they believe are beneath their abilities. These assignments may be the product of a transfer to a location with a more temperate climate or even a required tour in a department that is supposed to broaden the employee's experience. If self-motivation is lacking, then a position turns into a job, and a job turns into distasteful drudgery.

Managers seldom accept responsibility for employees who fail, even though it directly reflects on their own management capabilities. Some managers believe employees alone are liable for their own success or failurc. Managers may even naively appraise every assignment as an "opportunity." Here are some interesting ways managers can cause employees to fail:

- ⭢ Employees can fail because managers place them into positions in which they are likely to fail in the first place. In fact this is a favorite way to get rid of employees that managers want out of the business.
- ⭢ Employees can fail because managers dole out demanding assignments to people who do not possess the necessary skills. Some managers allow no time for training and expect their employees to learn on-the-job, even though this may cause inferior output. Too often a cop-out philosophy of "the strong survive and the weak shall perish" is utilized to supplant a lack of management talent.
- ⭢ Employees can fail because the assignment was not adequately defined or because its meaning changed with time. Employees really get upset with this kind of experience, especially if management holds the worker to a meaningless schedule.
- ⭢ Employees can fail because managers make unrealistic commitments for their employees.

It is extremely important to recognize the symptoms in employees that accompany pending failures. A brooding attitude, unappreciated humor, and avoided encounters (leads to voluntary isolation) are a few of the signs of an unhappy trooper. Perhaps there is denial. But even excellent employees occasionally fail. It is unrealistic to think employees will never encounter tribulations in their careers. Be prepared, and accept this as part of life. Make the unpleasant experience as short as possible.

It is far better to blunder early in your career, because a defeat is difficult to accept in a career in which you have only achieved repeated success. Veteran employees have been known to break under the stress of a first adversity. Nevertheless, it is best to admit you are failing and ask for help. You may even be rewarded for exposing a disaster; managers do not like surprises.

Starting Over with a Different Manager

Whenever employees are assigned new managers (even in the same organization), the employees' past accomplishments can be almost forgotten. What may count instead is the job level, and like in all big bureaucratic organizations, a job description exists to explain the duties of employees at that level. Workers may have to prove themselves all over again. The theme of such an attitude seems to be, "What have you done recently?" Actually, this is good for the employee and the company. Workers can't rest on their laurels, and special relationships with prior managers are voided.

The sin of most management people in this situation is that they don't take the time to review the qualifications, accomplishments, or general backgrounds of their newly assigned employees. Human Resources delights in the existence of the personnel jacket, which contains all relevant employee information. It's a well-known packet, so managers cannot use the excuse that these data are non-existent or inconvenient to obtain. Managers put stuff in the personnel jackets (for example, during yearly performance reviews) but rarely bother to take stuff out and read it.

Humor in the Workplace

One of the best tools employees can use to cope with the day-to-day tribulations of working for a large corporation is to develop a finely tuned sense of humor. However, the time, the place, and the subject matter of humor should be carefully chosen to reduce the potential for unknowingly offending someone. For example, when individuals cannot accept tasteful fun directed at themselves, then avoid making them the objects of your wit because you will only succeed in creating adversaries. For workplace humor to succeed, people need to laugh with you. In addition, being able to laugh at yourself is a sign of maturity that can be used to your advantage. It shows that you are not easily agitated and do not have an exaggerated ego.

Some people in management interpret humor as a distraction from getting the job done. They fail to recognize its pleasant side effects, such as relieving tension or deflecting the hostility of a competing group. But lack of humor in the workplace can lead to uptight attitudes that make an eight-hour day seem like endless drudgery. Difficult situations can be disarmed with simple, ironic statements like "Isn't this fun?" or "Aren't we having fun?" Everyone knows times are tough, so saying the opposite somehow lessens the severity. Managers should realize that well-placed wit can have a more positive effect on productivity than most motivational talks.

However, at times humor needs to be tempered with common sense:

⊷ Meeting high-level management for the first time is an event that demands formality. Generally, first impressions last a long time. This is one time to be serious.

⊷ Don't joke with your manager during an unfavorable performance evaluation.

⊷ Refrain from congratulating a promoted employee with humor that can be taken several ways. This detracts from the achievement and may label you as a poor loser.

Peaks and Valleys

Most professional work environments create unplanned demands on their people as a matter of course. It sometimes becomes an accepted method of operation to work fanatically on one day only to find the following days void of any challenges to occupy your time. These conditions can last for days, months, and even years.

Sometimes workers marvel that other similarly employed individuals are experiencing slack time while they are working themselves to death. Occasionally this occurs because of poor management, but it may be just the nature of the job. This situation frequently occurs because employees are reacting to external forces beyond their control, such as relying on outside commitments that don't materialize, responding to queries that would normally be handled by someone who has taken ill or is on vacation, and preparing a presentation that the manager needs for an unexpected trip out of town. However, panic days also occur because of poor planning, unrealistic estimating, or other circumstances over which individuals do exercise some control. Make an effort to point out errors of peer or management judgment that will adversely affect you. Seldom will a panic day end when an employee leaves the office. The thoughts usually linger until more recent events take their place of importance in the employee's memory.

During the ideal workday, minimal intrusions invade an individual's expected activities. There should be no surprises, yet there always are. Therefore, plan for interruptions, and if they don't materialize, then experience pleasant surprise. If managers are responsible for the hysteria, they have been known to say, "This will never happen again." If you hear this, realize the statement is meant to appease your present panic with the hope that you will accommodate the unpleasantness for the duration. Management really means that it desires to minimize future unexpected conditions. You, of course, should realize that if the demands of the business require panic days again, then such well-meaning rhetoric may be forgotten or even denied.

These disagreeable intrusions and slack workdays are collectively known as peaks and valleys. You may wonder why there is always a buzzword to associate with something you may be experiencing for the first time. It's because although the condition seems new to you, it's been around for a long time. Employees need to recognize that peaks and valleys occur just like business cycles. Come to know the symptoms before they occur so you can plan life outside work accordingly.

You should take advantage of a valley to acquire new skills, take deferred vacation, or look for another job. Rewards for surviving peak times seldom occur when the peak is happening, so stick around to collect what's owed. The rumor mill should serve as a guide for timing such a move. Management even recognizes that employees need a rest after a particularly demanding work schedule. Management's customary solutions include enrolling in a company-sponsored class, taking time off in lieu of monetary compensation, or taking a tour of duty in a less-pressing job.

In addition, you should take advantage of a peak to show what you can do under pressure. Your reputation hinges on that outcome whether you realize it or not. Panic situations often reveal the true characters of your fellow workers, so remember what they (most likely) unknowingly disclose. You may not get another opportunity to find out what your peers are made of. (By the way, the integrity of your employer will also be revealed.) Use the peak as a bargaining chip in future salary discussions. Surviving such an experience will also automatically increase the bond with your peers that comes with seeing things through to successful completion.

People Impressions and Evaluations

In a dynamic organization, employees encounter new acquaintances as a matter of course. You will come to appreciate the opinions and insight of some of these people, while their opposites will promote a false image of being the center of the knowledge universe. In actuality the majority of workers fall between these contrasting types. How can you tell who's who? Concentrate on the inner qualities of individuals, because what's inside reflects on the outside. Look for actions that reflect personal traits like honesty, commitment, intelligence, and motivation. These qualities endure. They reveal integrity. Remember that training and education can be acquired relatively easily, while character formation occurs in the early years of life and is intensely elusive later on. Catchy buzzwords, forced smiles, happy handshakes, and physical dress can serve as specious substitutes for a person's true character. Yet these are the criteria a lot of individuals depend on for choosing associates, collaborators, and allies. Character substance recognized during a first encounter generally proves correct. So don't be afraid to make these kinds of unspoken, private judgments. Store this evaluation for future reference.

How can this knowledge help you, as an employee? For starters, you can make decisions about meeting attendance depending on who the participants are, as well as the subject matter. Don't waste time on people whose purpose is to put on a show or impress others with surface information. Trust the opinions of those whom you, in turn, trust. Select associates who will do what they say. Even if you must work alongside someone who does not meet your unwritten standards for a desirable peer, you can make allowances to compensate for suspected deficiencies. Often, just knowing how someone will react in given situations can work to your advantage. Expectations are realistic, conflicts can be avoided, and surprises are detoured. These things all make the work experience more palatable.

Some employees delight in saying they wear two hats. One is worn at work, while the other is more suited for the home. This means they can change appearances depending on the situation. Nevertheless it remains difficult to change what's on the inside. Knowing what's inside a worker peer almost guarantees that you will not be misled by external show.

In the end, all individuals must make decisions about the people they meet. All situations require evaluation, insight, and judgment. Outside the work environment, these same individuals subconsciously select classmates, friends, and family by using mental processes they may not even know they employ. The possession of perceptive appraisal skills is an extremely desirable quality. Some call this subliminal assessment a gut feeling. Trust it. It usually works.

Burnout

Why do people sometimes experience gradual disinterest in their jobs, which then leads to the popular state of burnout? Who is to blame? What should an individual do who admits to such a condition? Burnout candidates are usually high-level performers possessing an extreme sense of commitment. They work long and hard with an end goal of achieving success in reputation, compensation, social status, and even work for work's sake. Everything revolves around the job. Family, social events, and even their basic religious beliefs can take a backseat whenever these people's lives are so dominated. People can even form emotional attachments to jobs. They may become obsessed with the pressure, excitement, sense of accomplishment, and visibility of particularly challenging projects.

Symptoms leading to cases of burnout include the following:

- Being willing to work unplanned/extensive overtime even though it means missing an important event with friends or family
- Excessively using work-related jargon in environments outside work
- Habitually coming to work early and leaving after normal quitting time
- Taking a trip out of town on short notice
- Abandoning logic and believing the corporation can do no wrong
- Following the career advancements of others, especially peer employees
- Believing that only you are capable of doing the best job
- Not taking lunch, coffee breaks, or other company-approved time away from work

When burnout occurs, people often reverse their attitudes about their current jobs and toward life outside the workplace. They take a long-term view, re-evaluate career goals, and justify adjustments toward that end. Perhaps for the first time, they take time to think about what's important and what's not important. They may even conclude that they need a totally different way to make a living. Look at burnout as a new beginning, not the end that people have associated with this situation.

Of course certain economic conditions may prevent immediate action. Also be aware that burnout will affect your job performance. Company management simply does not tolerate workers who are not performing at 100 percent. It makes no difference what you did in the past. So try and maintain a semblance of adequate achievement while you ponder your next step.

Remember that while a career does need to give the employee some degree of satisfaction, it is really just a method of obtaining money so you can enjoy things and people outside the work environment. Therefore, in the end the individual employee must assume responsibility for burnout. So choose priorities wisely when a choice is available. Balance other things in life that are more lasting, more meaningful. Be willing to shift priorities to maintain your sense of what's important.

Conclusion

As an employee in a large corporation, you must learn to correctly decipher the many diverse incidents that occur in order to maintain the proper perspective about what's really happening. The true intent of the events, organizations, and procedures is sometimes elusive because it is often disguised in euphemistic words and actions. Avoid unpleasantness and surprises by looking beneath the surface of what is obvious. Develop a keen insight so that your working days will be less frustrating and more productive. You will find you can sometimes predict the future thanks to your honed skill of perception.

A Look at Management

~ or ~

I May Be Ineffective, But I Have a Nice Office

Sometimes you may wonder exactly why a management structure is necessary in corporations. It can be argued that some managers get in the way more than they contribute to the output of their particular areas of responsibility. Some managers irritate employees with incessant meddling. Others attempt to represent their employees' efforts to others but inevitably mess it up. Some compete with their workers on a technical level to show everyone that they could still do real work if they had to. In fact this competition tends to erode the trust that is so necessary between managers and their employees. Managers mostly perform administrative functions; rarely are they called upon to make decisions that affect the future of their departments.

The real value of managers is to assign work to individuals who they believe can do the job and then get out of their way. A hovering manager slows down the work effort and contributes to the cover-yourself attitude that then prevails. Managers should also keep the outside world from disturbing the activities of their departments so meaningful work can be accomplished. But some managers rarely do what they should do. Instead, they constantly search for ways to make themselves more visible to further their careers rather than realizing that if their employees successfully turned out superior products, those managers would be recognized as the catalysts who made that happen.

Because most organizations are pyramidal in structure, game playing can become important among people vying for their next management promotions. The higher they rise, the more competitive the game is. Mostly the competition is political in nature with little effect on the well-being of the company's income or growth. In other words, in large organizations, perception rather than reality usually propels people into higher levels of management. Finally their rise may stop because someone else is better at the game playing. Consequently, they may be stuck in jobs that they either don't want or don't know how to do. This is especially true of fast trackers whose meteoric rise never required them to be responsible for doing anything.

Some managers of managers have even less real work to do, so these people often bombard their subordinates with questions, reviews, requests for reports, and other things so they can gain a sense of contribution. In fact most of what these people do is to make work for others. Many upper-level managers tend to associate only with individuals of their same rank or higher and thus often lose communication with those who know the straight skinny. They can become further and further removed from reality and may begin to function in a world full of rumors and half-truth information. They may claim that their positions have a great deal of responsibility when in fact, if they were somehow incapacitated, probably no one would miss them, and the department's work output might be better than ever. This occasionally happens, but then the company usually tries to find a position of importance for the defrocked manager because of the unwritten corporate rule that says, "Once a manager, a manager forever."

In this day of hiring contractors to supplement the company's work force, hiring temporary managers would make even more sense because they would not owe any debts to other managers for their positions and would therefore be free to make sure what they were hired to do actually happened. Outside managers would bring a fresh perspective to a world of inbred management. Just like direct subcontractors, they would be terminated once the workload decreased. Later, contract managers could even be offered permanent jobs in the company because of their accomplishments.

The Making of Management

Corporate management sometimes creates the illusion that only ambitious, bright, aggressive employees are selected for management positions. However, a large percentage of employees view management as a boring, non-creative, administrative task. Managers must take care of dull things like:

- ◆ Evaluating their employees
- ◆ Getting them raises
- ◆ Seeing that they have the tools to do their jobs
- ◆ Attending regular meetings about such elusive topics as strategy, direction, and equal opportunity
- ◆ Keeping records of employee overtime, vacation, sick days, time cards, and so on
- ◆ Warding off critics

These types of jobs often consume managers' time so they cannot contribute to the efforts of their departments. Sometimes the previously listed items appeal to employees who find the notion of performing real, measurable work intimidating. In addition, these people may realize that playing the management game is more financially rewarding than doing their current work. Therefore, early in their careers, these management wannabes make it known that they would rather coordinate the efforts of others. They may convince themselves they can affect the company more by directing others than by being responsible for their own work. This belief may be accurate if these individuals also possess leadership qualities. However, real leaders do so by example, not by holding the title of manager. Sadly, in today's world, too many individuals aspire to become managers when they realize they do not possess the skills, discipline, or endurance to do their assigned tasks effectively over time. It's as if people become managers by default. Consequently, by becoming managers, people can advance based on the work done by others rather than their own efforts alone.

Those in charge of doling out management positions should evaluate candidates based on their ability to lead, not administrate. It's unfortunate that managers in power often pick management candidates who mirror their own characteristics. This can quickly lead to a breeding ground for incompetent managers. However, when the most competent candidates are reluctant to become managers, the financial incentives for taking that first step are usually not sufficient to sway that decision. The company's alternative is often to give the managerial job to anyone willing to accept it. When this happens, the practice expressed by the adage, "Once a manager, a manager forever" usually permits the incompetent to rise in the power structure of a corporation. This is one reason why executives of large corporations usually are no match for leaders of small companies, who attained their positions by being true leaders.

Management Selection

One effective way to be chosen for the management game is to state this interest to those who exert influence in the selection process, as does the employee who constantly says, "Make me a manager! Make me a manager!" ad nauseam. This expression of desire seems to be one of the most important qualifications for entering the ranks of those who direct, administer, evaluate, and monitor. Although this verbalization may irritate his fellow workers, it plants a seed in current management's thoughts that employee Joe Wannabe wants to coordinate the activities of others rather than work at the lower level. A noble aspiration. But in reality, Joe may know he is only a mediocre worker, and therefore he may feel he must isolate himself from performing any measurable work. Meetings, employee performance evaluations, strategy sessions, and so on will henceforth consume Joe's time, and Joe knows it and loves it. Rarely is an individual chosen for management without vocalizing such a desire.

In most companies, it also is equally important for management-aspiring employees to advertise their performance in their present positions. For example, employee Wendy Wannabe, who continually advertises a heavy workload, numerous hours of overtime, and the number of problems assigned to her, gives the impression of deep commitment. In fact, she would like everyone to think most of the department's work passes through her hands. Conversely, when individuals work diligently every day without fanfare, this may work against them. Why? When employees can solve anything that comes across their desks, the perception may be generated that their jobs are routine—even though they may be great problem solvers. Individuals, in effect, have to mount campaigns to publicize their desired goal of a management position.

Sometimes employees are asked to take management positions even though they have expressed no interest in such a job. The reason often becomes clear when these employees look at the departments they have been asked to manage. Usually, the departments are in crisis mode (low morale, hopelessly behind schedule, workers quitting the company), and management may need some sacrificial lambs to shield those responsible from the mess. The unfortunate sacrificial lambs may be told that they are being given a great opportunity, challenge, or whatever—just so they agree to be placed between the chaos and upper management. Sometimes they succeed in turning the departments around and—guess what—they are usually given charge of other situations that smell of failure. Subsequently, the good old boys in management may begin to feel uneasy because the new managers are showing them up. Entrenched management may secretly wish for their demise. As you can see, worker-type managers who don't campaign for a management slot usually make the best managers.

Another type of employee who becomes a manager is the technical guru who thinks he knows everything. He is usually selected for management because executives assume that his success in one area assures his success in others. Unfortunately, this employee usually doesn't know anything about motivating or getting along with people. He usually thinks he can do the job better than anyone else, and he may tell his employees this. He competes with members of his department in almost everything— even when the result doesn't matter. This can result in alienation, low morale, and defection of department members. Luckily, this type of individual is usually smart enough to decide to return to a productive life as a contributing worker employee.

When middle management wants a virtual puppet whom it can control in a managerial slot, then it often selects an individual who does not have strong opinions of her own, who is agreeable in order to avoid confrontation, or who will cater to her superiors for personal gain. This happens too often and points out the insecurities of mid-level managers who promote such people to these positions. Meetings can provide an interesting forum to witness this subservience in the form of such phrases as, "I agree with the statement of Joe Mid-Level Manager," or "Joe Mid-Level Manager is more knowledgeable on the subject than I." Unfortunately, puppet managers can last a long time in large organizations. Puppets usually only feel uneasy when they realize their godfather is in trouble. Then they may demonstrate a remarkable turnaround in their behavior. They may begin to distance themselves from the falling star mid-level manager and openly disagree with his or her decisions. This does not go unnoticed in the ranks of the worker employees, and it usually signals that a reorganization is forthcoming.

Managers with the responsibility of designating their replacements may bring in one of their associates. This is because the managers have already established working relationships with these individuals, which usually guarantees their gratitude and continued loyalty. If large numbers of managers are selected, then the inbreeding of new managers who emulate their godfather may be even more noticeable because of the sheer numerical size. Coattailing is simply a fact of life in most large corporations because the immediate effect of a new manager is not evident for some time. Learning the management job can take years, and meanwhile the workers continue to toil hard because they want to impress the new leader. No other employees in a company are cut so much slack in proving themselves as managers are.

Ever wonder why wholesale management changes often occur whenever a high-level manager is replaced? Simple: The new top dog may know his underlings are loyal to his predecessor, so he may bring in his own crew, who he knows will be loyal to him.

Once a manager is placed in her new position, be cautious because several things can happen. First, she may embark on an ego inflation trip, especially if the position went to an outside-the-company individual. She may tell the workers of her exploits, and of course, all have successful conclusions. She may use certain phrases to impress employees, such as, "I'm from the advanced systems space." Exactly what does the word *space* mean? It doesn't matter; it sounds impressive, and she may continue to use catchy phrases to further mystify people with her brilliance. Seasoned veterans, however, have heard it all many times before. Hence, this new manager usually only succeeds in alienating her experienced employees. Second, the new manager may busy herself with attending meetings so she can be recognized as the new person in control. Unfortunately, these meetings probably have more to do with ensuring her success than with doing a good job. This is where political skills can really pay off and why talented people can become disillusioned with the day-to-day operations of a large corporation. Third, the manager may believe she can manage anything, and therefore she may never bother to understand what is going on. She may use charts, schedules, meetings, and so on as her method of management. To this type of manager, it just doesn't seem to matter if a project is of any value to the company's customers, as long as it's on schedule and within cost projections.

Why and How a Manager?

With all the flak management takes these days, why do individuals continue to aspire to such positions? Recognition, status, power, money, perks, flexibility, and travel all help make any indignity suffered in this capacity seem worthwhile. However, it is considered in bad taste to list any of the aforementioned attributes as reasons to become a manager. If you have this aspiration, your real thinking in this matter should be kept to yourself. Instead, people who want to become managers have been known to give the following reasons (which cannot be easily measured):

- ☙ "The opportunity to have a larger impact."
- ☙ "The opportunity to make better use of my skills."
- ☙ "The opportunity to lead other employees."
- ☙ "The opportunity to influence the direction of the company."

So if you want to be a manager, make your rationale sound positive, benevolent, inspiring, and even visionary. Also remember that only managers select future managers, so it is wise to emulate those in power. Start dressing the part even before you know you are being considered for a management position. In effect, you need to campaign for an opening as if you were running for public office.

As an aspiring manager, skills in verbalization can be more important than any technical skill you might possess. I didn't use the more global term *communication skills,* for that phrase encompasses written thought, and anything written is difficult to change. A large number of managers survive because they can talk their way out of any situation. Even if they said something incorrect, these managers can change the true meaning by rephrasing statements in a different tense, person, plurality, context, and so on.

Once the mantle of management is bestowed, individuals often separate themselves from the non-management work force. This aspect seems to be a carryover from the 1800s, which featured a distinct difference in the educational level attained by supervisory and non-supervisory personnel. However, some managers do survive, prosper, and feel good about themselves because they treat people like they want to be treated.

A Look at Some Management Styles

In any large organization, the personalities of its members determine the quality of the work environment. Don't be intimidated by managers who display offensive attributes. Take comfort in knowing that others have experienced similar circumstances.

Dedicated employees tend to emulate perceived successful people in the organization. Witness the example of the successful railroad tycoon of the late 1800s. The lifestyles and habits of cigar smoking, pot-bellied executives were widely copied by aspiring wannabes. Here is a collection of management personalities to help you decide whom to copy and whom to look out for.

The Crude Manager

The personality traits of the crude manager include extreme boldness, insolence, and disrespect. An intimidated management staff often misinterprets these characteristics as signs of an aggressive leader. In the more advanced stages, such a manager relies on gutter English vocabulary to intimidate subordinates. Too often these underlings incorporate the same language style, approaching the vulgarity of the crude manager. Such emulated behavior flatters this ill-mannered manager and often impresses those inexperienced in such tactics. However, the effect of this conduct on individuals of good breeding is usually to shun both the coarse leader and his followers. The effect on the company is that it does not realize the benefit of the talents of such alienated employees. However, as most people come to understand, crude management can last for years because:

- The ill-mannered manager has a godfather who protects him from detractors.
- The ill-mannered manager is not responsible for anything that can be measured, so success or failure is not easy to detect.
- The ill-mannered manager possesses great skill at *managing upward*. (This term is generally applied to an individual who appears amiable and competent to his superiors while at the same time is totally unfit to manage those who report to him.)
- The ill-mannered manager promises the moon but never has to deliver. So he looks good while doing nothing.

Coping with a personality of this type is somewhat difficult. Above all, it is never wise to stoop to the same level. Remember that such a person is a master of the direct insult. He is able to instantly verbalize degrading comments. This ploy is meant to distract your focus during any discussion with him and is thus effective whenever varying points of view surface. So you should maintain a calm, composed exterior. This demeanor may even irritate the crude manager. An unperturbed employee is able to deflect caustic barrages of indignities, and such a reaction implies that she is not upset by such behavior. Avoidance is another useful strategy that contributes to the isolation of the offensive manager. It also makes an employee's workday more pleasant. If a sufficient number of your fellow workers adopt this avoidance method, the lack of communication will reduce the effectiveness of the crude manager. However, avoidance is not possible if he is judged (by a unenlightened management staff) to be a key player in the company's operation. In this case, do your homework and factually critique any barbs directed at you or your assigned project. Do it from a distance (third person, copy list, and so on), for this implies that you are too busy to be bothered by the antics of an unimportant detractor. Eventually, all bad things come to an end.

If a crude manager is a cog in the communication wheel by which you receive information necessary to do your job, find another source. Do not depend on an irritant for any communication because you run the risk of becoming out-of-date by your avoidance of the unpleasant personality.

Sometimes upper management uses a crude subordinate manager to further its own agenda. It's kind of like the good-guy/bad-guy scenario employed by law enforcement. Upper management may feel the need to maintain its appearance as the benevolent employer, so it may leave the unpleasant task of irritating workers into a state of urgency to the crude manager. This method allows upper management to skillfully avert any hard feelings while maintaining the good-guy image. Frequently an offensive manager is discarded because he has succeeded too well at the unofficial task of irritating his fellow (or superior) workers. His galling tactics knew no bounds. Also, instead of the sought-after sense of urgency, he may have instilled a sense of apathy because of the widespread belief that such a job is not worth the aggravation.

The Communicating and Non-communicating Managers

By formally and informally communicating with employees who perform the actual work, managers establish a rapport that positively affects morale and gives a sense of importance to employees, promoting the idea that their opinions and efforts count. Non-communicating managers often allot periods in their work week to officially share information with their employees. The very act of parceling out such time indicates that a serious deficiency exists in that manager's people skills. Weekly departmental meetings that happen regardless of if there is anything to discuss are a well-known manifestation of this practice. Information sharing should not be an event that is scheduled but rather one that occurs as a normal part of everyday work experience. A manager who communicates well spends less time isolating herself in her office. Being a desk manager is one path that leads to failure.

Communication comes in many flavors. Words spoken in the presence of others, as well as private kudos written in personal notes, all have a positive effect on an employee's work ethic. When a higher-level manager communicates directly with workers at the lowest levels, this deed pays huge dividends. The grapevine soon lets everyone know that such a manager is to be treated with respect and loyalty.

Open communication ultimately saves time in the workplace. Mistakes caused by assumptions, guesses, and outdated information are reduced, and the effort to fix these kinds of errors can be used toward doing something else.

Excessive documentation is often used to substitute for good communication. Written information produced in solitude expresses a single point of view. It cannot substitute for verbal interchange, which allows people with multiple viewpoints to reach a shared conclusion in a short period of time. When this verbal interchange occurs, the participants now have a stake in that outcome.

In addition, communication is a double-edged sword. If a manager freely discusses items relating to work (or any item for that matter), she will find that her employees more readily share their experiences regarding the progress and problems associated with assigned tasks. Good communicators are good listeners. The frequently quoted phrase, "I never learned anything by talking" is quite appropriate in this situation. Such information exchanges contribute to an atmosphere of informality. A job that incorporates attitudes of friendliness, familiarity, and simplicity makes happy employees.

Therefore, managers should remember that the net result of good two-way communication is that people work harder and are willing to endure hardships (overtime, tight deadlines, and so on) because of their relationship with management. They believe the company cares because it is willing to listen, as well as administer.

The Condescending Manager

Unfortunately, some managers see themselves as so superior to their workers that they subconsciously want their employees to know this. These managers delight in engaging in one-upsmanship techniques, in which the viewpoints of the managers always prevail. Although this behavior may boost the egos of such managers, it detracts from the output of individuals who feel put down. The affected workers often retaliate by only putting forth an effort that meets the requirements of the job. The manager's dress, speech, viewpoints, and mannerisms (like hand expressions, sarcastic humor, lighting up a cigarette, vending machine etiquette, and so on) can all contribute to creating an air of superiority. This type of manager has never learned that successful managers lead by example.

Valid contributions made by others in a department may be unfairly downgraded by a manager who deems himself above his department members. His ego just won't let him admit that other people have something to say too. Worse yet, a condescending manager may assimilate a portion of a subordinate's notoriety by associating himself with that subordinate's successful accomplishment. Phrases such as "under my direction" and "I recognized the importance of . . ." detour a portion of the recognition to the manager, who then uses such undeserved remarks to his advantage. Subordinate accomplishments tend to surface under different names that relate in some way to the manager's prior accomplishments. The achievements of others may even be massaged to incorporate the personal slant (for example, universal applicability or worldwide ramifications) of a manager who believes he is destined for bigger things. In a large corporation, aspiring workers often willingly share the repute of their achievements with people who have more visible positions. Sometimes this route is necessary for workers to gain acceptance within the company bureaucracy, even though their achievements may be able to stand on their own merits.

It is not easy to work with a condescending manager. Unfortunately, the employee's desire to minimize personal discussion, debate, confrontation, or whatever with a patronizing manager can lead to a situation of assumed agreement, in which others perceive that the manager is always right. Therefore, endure some discomfort by always stating your views with clarity and confidence. Popularize your perspective to others, especially if you are clearly right. Encourage others to challenge the overbearing manager. Perhaps he will tire under the stress of such organized opposition.

Other unpleasant consequences also may occur when you, the employee, are dominated by an overbearing manager. His way, his interpretation, or his assumptions may place your confidence in jeopardy. This can greatly subdue your questioning attitude. You may find yourself unable to function without explicit directions from your superior. Never let yourself get into this predicament.

One of the favorite expressions used by a contemptuous person (manager or peer) is, "I would explain it to you, but you probably wouldn't understand it anyway." In other words, he is saying you are too stupid to comprehend. To utter such a phrase is a sign of extreme malice. Whenever individuals hear it for the first time, they may be so taken aback by this absurd comment that they will probably fail to rebut the remark with a simple, "Try me" or "I think I can handle it." Is it any wonder that personality conflicts seem to accompany the condescending manager?

The Technically Involved Manager

Different employees require different management styles (or combinations thereof). Technically involved managers are best suited to act as mentors for new and/or inexperienced workers. They guide, assist, advise, critique, and otherwise directly affect the actions of their employees. They assume the role of teachers who just happen to be managers. This works quite well for this class of workers. However, the exact same style utilized in a department of experienced people can have disastrous results. Seasoned workers may look at this excessive direction as a lack of confidence in their ability to do their assignments. Managers must constantly adapt to succeed and recognize when the situation requires a different approach. This is one reason why a given manager can be both hated and held in esteem at the same time: She assumed that one-size-fits-all would work in all situations.

Some people cannot let go of the jobs they had before becoming managers. This attribute applies to successful worker types who need to know everything that is going on. This method of operation can arise from being insecure to refusing to believe that others can actually perform a task without constant direction. These hands-on managers often fail to appreciate the fact that others are paid to do the actual work while a manager is paid to administrate and to motivate, guide, and defend her departmental employees. This type of manager usually doesn't last long because she eventually becomes so busy doing several jobs that she runs out of gas, while her employees languish for lack of meaningful assignments.

Companies should never promote a technical employee to manage her former department. Debts owed to her former peers, bitterness because of a lost competition, and even subordinates' knowledge that their former co-worker has access to their personnel jackets all can contribute to lack of acceptance. It is best to install a new manager in an area that is removed from her former department.

The Manager As a Friend

One of the most successful management styles is to gain the confidence and respect of *select* employees by becoming their friend. This type of relationship can pay huge dividends. From the employees' point of view, they participate in honest communication without the mind games that people in supervision like to play. For example, if an upcoming manager-sanctioned meeting has the potential of turning into a political morass, individuals chosen to attend can discreetly inform their supervisors of their suspicions without fear of being labeled non-team players (this tag is like an ecclesiastical curse in a big company), habitual skeptics, or other patronizing titles. The employees gain because they can spend their efforts accomplishing meaningful tasks. They realize a sense of accomplishment. The company gains because its employees are more productive. The managers also gain because they do not have to waste time trying to convince their subordinate-friends that such a meeting has value.

Nevertheless, most individuals in the management game shun friendship associations because of the potential loss of objectivity. Of course this point of view has validity. Befriended employees can take advantage of this association by not putting out their best effort. However, this is unlikely because people usually become friends because they admire qualities in each other. A manager wouldn't consciously befriend an employee who is a poor performer. Employees wouldn't befriend a manager whom they do not respect. This mutual evaluation occurs before any commitment to friendship is even considered. People who are friends work better together than people who are forced together in the normal boss-worker organization. Companies seem to endorse a carryover attitude from the military that says, "It doesn't pay to be friends with subordinates because you may have to order them to participate in a life-threatening situation." This kind of impersonal, one-size-fits-all supervision thinking needs to be reassessed in the context of the modern corporation.

The Quiet Manager

Some people are quiet by nature. This managerial attribute is generally preferred by employees who dislike noisy people who talk just to command attention. A person's reticent personality can be the result of a belief that it is rude to talk when there is nothing to say. When a quiet person speaks, perceptive people listen because they realize that the occasion usually reveals meaningful information.

Having a successful career as a college student does not mean that success will follow in the corporate world. Scholarly competence is rewarded with good grades. Written tests that gauge knowledge determine grades. Talk is cheap in academia. There are no "weasel words" that substitute for knowing the correct answer. In the corporate world, the tests are meeting a schedule, producing quality work, and so on. But these measurable entities tend to blur when people accept the position of manager. At this level a manager is gauged not by what he actually does but by the efforts of the employees in his department. Recognizing that he has nothing directly measurable to do, some managers find themselves with a lot of time on their hands. What choices exist to promote their careers in management? Simple: The verbose manager (who is in the majority) gets to talk about stuff rather than having to do it. The best talk-manager may appear as a visionary of the first order. It often doesn't matter if the things he verbalizes never come to pass. To this person, the art of the bluff will likely become a prized possession and a necessary tool for advancement. The stuff that he promises will happen may be surrounded with nice-sounding phrases that disguise the true state of progress. How does the quiet manager survive in such an environment?

Usually reserved individuals don't last long in an organization if they are incompetent because their spoken words are thoroughly analyzed. In addition quiet managers usually don't believe in the talk game. Such personalities may even scorn those who make a living by abusing the spoken word. To a department employee, the real danger in having a quiet individual as a manager is that he may not adequately represent the real contributions of his people to the outside world. Raises and promotions may not occur as frequently in the quiet manager's department as in a department managed by an individual who is skilled in the art of verbal communication. As a result, some competent individuals tend to avoid working for such an overly restrained person. This kind of manager needs to understand the necessity of a verbal offense in required situations.

Quiet managers usually survive and advance by earning a reputation for doing what they said they would do. The workday is filled with removing obstacles that would prevent their department from fulfilling any commitments. They become adept at bypassing verbose peers and are content in just doing a good job. Additionally, non-wordy managers need to be politically astute because their lack of a verbal facade leaves them vulnerable to situations in which an unanswered word assault can give imprecise and even false impressions.

All in all, quiet managers are right about at least one thing: Most of the time it is better to listen than talk.

The Boisterous Manager

Loud, noisy managers often act this way because they feel a need to dominate a conversation. They are also usually good with words, and they promote this trait by speaking so all can hear. Such individuals usually are rowdy by nature, but some acquire this demeanor because they witness the career advantages demonstrated by an active practitioner. The bull-in-a-china-shop behavior is tolerated because many administrators think ambitious people should behave this way. However, an exterior of turbulence is often used to mask feelings of insecurity.

The boisterous manager believes loud noise is useful as a defense mechanism because it prevents others from expressing their views. Her opponents never get a chance to be heard even if they speak. Drowning out an adversary by blaring discourse is especially effective in meetings to demonstrate resolve. Somehow loudness has become equated with the degree of truth. (This perception is false.) Unfortunately, many upper-level managers are easily impressed by verbal dominance.

How can you survive a boisterous manager? First, avoid her if her behavior offends you. Second, never try to outtalk this kind of individual. She is a master at the game of one-upsmanship. Third, becoming a target of a loud verbal attack is unpleasant even if the words are untrue. However, it is extremely important to counter any undeserved criticism because your reputation could suffer. Use means other than verbal debate to correct a false impression created by a loud manager. A brief terminating remark or a factual memo with the correct copy list works quite well. In practice, employees of such a manager tend to withdraw into turn-off mode when bombarded by the continued verbal blasts.

A boisterous manager always has a story to tell, and it's never short. The business world likes to refer to these tales as scenarios or vignettes. Somehow these words have a more transcendental appeal. They also lend a degree of veracity. The stories are usually somewhat humorous because the manager needs to believe that people enjoy hearing such tales. Employees even find this kind of manager entertaining at times. Often the tales concern past adventures and work experiences that are intended to impress listeners. Her boasts of achievements often stretch truth to limits that test believability. However, this does not deter the loud manager's resolve to dominate verbal communication.

However, a boisterous manager does give her department some useful things, for example:

- The activities of her employees are continually advertised. Perhaps this occurs because such a manager thinks of her department as an extension of herself. Nevertheless, this popularity aids in securing raises and promotions for her employees because others are continually made aware of each and every accomplishment.
- Noisy managers are good at shifting the blame for any setback away from their departments because criticism is deflected by boisterous and intimidating oratory.
- Employees of a loud manager gain experience that is useful in dealing with diverse personalities. Tolerating unpleasant situations thickens the skin, which hides or removes feelings of sadness that accompany personal affronts. (Never reveal your true inner self to an adversary for then she would know how to get to you.)

The Cover-Your-Anatomy Manager

Some people manage by cover-your-anatomy (CYA) mode in case something associated with an individual's department happens to go wrong. In practice this style involves accumulating a trail of communicated or implied evidence (paper, e-mail, witnesses) that puts one's self in the best light possible. The collected details are carefully selected. This ensures that their potential revelation will present only the intended perspective. This mode of operation may even involve gathering damaging information about managerial contemporaries only to be used if the proper moment presents itself. Survivors have learned that it is not necessary to take a fall when others less astute at the CYA style of management can absorb it for them.

Examples of collected information include the following:

- Data showing missed dependency commitments that may contribute to a future schedule slippage. This includes both external (outside the department) and internal (within the department) promises.
- Data that demonstrate the poor quality of an external dependency. This may impact the manager's contribution to a product or service composed of many steps or pieces.
- Minutes of meetings favoring the CYA manager's point of view. (Perhaps the minutes show that another more risky alternative was chosen instead of one championed by the CYA manager.)

This style of management is strictly defensive in nature and inhibits most risk-taking ventures associated with a progressive management. CYA tactics have even evolved to more petty levels, which resort to pointing fingers at contemporaries and their organizations. This maneuver deflects criticism to people and departments who may not be aware that such stuff is even happening.

At the least, this tactic buys time to fix problems. Some managers who act this way do so because they are insecure in their real work environments. Other practitioners view CYA methods as just being good at the political aspect of management in a large corporation. Perhaps.

A lot of time and effort can be wasted performing this useless CYA task. It does absolutely nothing to contribute to the success of current assignments. If managers behave this way to members of their own departments, and the employees find out about it, then everyone begins to function in CYA mode. Almost nothing useful gets done. Unfortunately, the CYA manager type is plentiful and contributes to the inefficiencies found in big companies. The style is even more widespread in the higher ranks of management.

Remember that if certain managers (or any employee for that matter) have never done anything wrong (a CYA goal), then they probably haven't done anything either.

The By-the-Book Manager

People who manage by constantly relying on a set of company-sanctioned rules can have both a positive and negative effect on their employees. If an employee can rely on the fact that a superior manages this way, then she knows exactly where she stands in all situations. There is no guesswork, no unexpected moves. These managers endorse procedures, conventions, and scheduled meetings whether they are needed or not. They do not take risks because these are not outlined in the manager's manual. They do not pursue leadership because by-the-book managers are reluctant to pursue anything not formally approved. In fact it's kind of boring to work for a by-the-book manager. They survive because some upper-level managers like this kind of predictable personality. By-the-book managers are easily manipulated and non-confrontational. However, management can easily replace people who use a rule book as a constant crutch.

Instead, the successful manager uses the rule book as a set of guidelines, open to interpretation and selective enforcement in order to achieve results (see Pitfalls of the Manager's Manual, p. 135).

The Transparent Manager

Ever come across an individual who seems like an OK guy but just doesn't seem to succeed at work? Transparent managers fall into this category. I call them transparent because they contribute so little to their departments, they might as well not be there at all. Veteran workers know it is easy to look the managerial part without actually doing anything as long as you subscribe to the following:

> ✍ The proper use of a wardrobe separates those in supervision from the worker class. It can solicit respect when none is deserved.

↬ The use of catchy buzzwords and phrases can foster the illusion of knowing what's going on.

↬ Performing simulated work activities (such as forwarding e-mail and working late to compensate for arriving late) can make a manager look like he is doing something.

A transparent manager may also have a lot of interests outside the company, and he lets these endeavors take precedence over daily work responsibilities. He seems to always be on the phone checking the progress of these distractions (these may range from civic duties to discussions with his stockbroker). The ultimate transgression is that a transparent manager finally (most likely unknowingly) lets the supervision aspect of his position migrate to one of his trusted subordinates. In effect the transparent manager becomes a figurehead drawing a salary as an observer. He may have even been a real contributor at one time. Pretty soon other members of the department, sensing this change in authority, begin to resent the fact that the real manager never talks to them directly but instead manages through this surrogate employee. Any contribution by a department employee filters through the substitute manager. This can adversely affect raises, reputations, and promotions, causing resentment, which leads to low morale. Low morale breeds discontent and even rebellion. The quality of work output may begin to deteriorate, and internal schedules may be adversely affected. This unspoken arrangement can last for some time. Soon an external deliverable is missed by a member of the department. When this happens, workdays become extremely difficult to endure. It seems that everyone outside the department knows about the problem. All those involved are assumed to be at fault. Morale sinks even lower.

Now the manager-surrogate is under a lot of pressure to fix the problem. His behavior can become irrational. Thinking that overtime will quickly solve the missed commitment, he demands department employees work an extraordinary number of hours. It's unfortunate that those in control erroneously equate output with time spent on the job. This may be true for a labor-intensive job but can backfire when the job requires mental sharpness. Sometimes time away from work is better than time spent at work.

Often, an inexperienced surrogate manager's lack of people skills causes a total breakdown in communication. Now fixing anything gets very difficult, because department projects are generally cooperative ventures. As the transparent manager continues to rely on input from his chosen coordinator, he becomes totally useless. When he tries to salvage the missed commitment, his incompetence and unfamiliarity with what's going on betray him in meetings with people trying to fix the bad situation. The temptation to relax and avoid unpleasant situations eventually catches up with a manager who shields himself through a third party.

If you ever find yourself working for a transparent manager, find yourself another job as soon as possible. You will save yourself a lot of grief.

The Hovering Manager

Individuals who manage by constantly checking up on their employees exhibit their own insecurities by this very trait. They never seem to fully trust their employees. Excessive monitoring becomes ingrained in this style of management to the point that normal responsibilities are neglected. For example, good managers should help their employees grow in their jobs so they (the workers) can assume more responsible positions. In this situation, even the manager benefits because the contribution level of her employees increases. However, a hovering manager stifles this growth by emphasizing mundane tasks like weekly status reports, one-on-one briefings, planned activities, and copies of all correspondence. Some seasoned employees combat these distractions by allotting time in their schedule to accommodate such annoyances. Hard-line hoverers refuse to appreciate the subtle humor of this tactic.

In its advanced stages, the hovering effect limits individual thinking and action so as to satisfy the next series of questions coming from a Hovering Harriett. (Note that Hovering Harriett may also be known as Micro Mary in some circles.) It's as if the manager needs a warm fuzzy to get through the day. For most employees, this causes a loss of initiative and ultimately confidence because people are only concerned with having an answer (any answer) to satisfy the constant barrage of management inquiries. Harriett comes into a worker's office space without any warning and diverts the worker's attention to the topics she wants to discuss. This act minimizes a worker's ability to do any work. But Harriett has already convinced herself that she is actually helping by stimulating communication. Too bad. Rather than running interference for members of her department, a Hovering Harriett creates it. Most informed people applaud the belief that anything done in excess is usually harmful. Of all things, Harriett is not informed of this aspect.

The more conscientious an individual is, the more a hovering style can detract from his contributions. He wants to please his manager and thus regresses into the role of a supplier of information. He diverts his energies to the task of keeping his manager informed at all costs. He wants to be diligent in everything he does, so this aspect of the job eventually leads to tracking the activities of others. Soon tracking assumes more importance than performing assigned tasks. These monitoring activities may be sufficient to survive in a department managed by Harriett, but the worker's career eventually suffers because opportunities in other departments, and other companies, don't exist for employees who specialize in reporting what others do.

Maturity and experience are the only cures for this type of manager quirk. Ironically, some higher-level managers interpret hovering maneuvers as sound business practice. This appears to be a leftover from the days of a work force involved in mostly repetitive activities. Thinking employees resent managers who specialize in micro-management tactics.

The Know-it-all Manager

Management people who think they know it all are doomed to fail. They will always run into others who know more than they do. However, the hubris that accompanies this type of manager will prevent them from recognizing that fact. So instead, they will begin a long-term career decline because no one wants to associate with them. Unfortunately, higher-level management sometimes places know-it-all managers in slots of importance to stimulate others into action. "He will set a fire under the slackers," they say, but their own lack of management selection insight will contribute to a stagnating situation they thought they were improving. They want to believe that they have discovered a true "boy wonder." This doesn't work, however, because both the peer and subordinate reaction will be to shun such an unpleasant person.

Employees need to feel they are making a difference, but whenever Mike Know-It-All evaluates their contributions, he always has a "more appropriate way" of doing things. It's one thing to secretly possess such an opposing opinion of no value. It's quite another to say it to an employee or even to convey such an attitude. For starters, such an attitude erodes employee confidence, removes initiative, and promotes complacency. If left unchecked, Mike can turn a once-productive department into one that is just collecting a paycheck.

The Crisis Manager

Some individuals can't seem to make anything happen unless there's a real or imagined crisis. The crisis manager uses this technique to give employees a sense of urgency that is somehow meant to make them work harder. This may take the form of overtime, meetings, trips out of town, competitors' performance statistics, and so on. Some managers believe a crisis will generate pressure, and pressure begets concentration, and concentration means that things will get done faster. Now, doing things faster may actually cause poor quality work, but to the crisis manager, this doesn't seem important. The important thing is that deadlines are met, commitments honored, and the nose-to-the-grindstone image maintained.

A crisis may be real or imagined. To the unseasoned employee, an imaginary crisis has the same effect as a real one, but to savvy employees, an imaginary crisis is but another game that causes further erosion of the credibility of such managers. Some symptoms of an imaginary crisis are as follows:

- Other non-crisis-managed departments wonder why you are working so much overtime.
- The crisis manager does not participate in the overtime.
- Regularly scheduled meetings are still mandatory.
- A project's deadline could be met within normal work hours, but the manager is still quick to invoke the powers of mandatory overtime for employees.

New employees often get caught up in the excitement of deadlines, weekend work, and showing their management that they want to be part of the team. Teamwork is an excellent characteristic of a valued employee; however, when operating in an imagined crisis mode, the work environment may reflect the every-man-for-himself school of thought because of the tremendous pressure to get something/anything done. Conversely, a real and believable crisis can generate a bond that fosters teamwork.

The Manager Who Was in the Military

People who spend time in the military never forget that experience, so some veterans tend to manage by issuing orders. Their everyday dress is impeccable, and their posture looks like they are on a parade ground—even when they are just walking to the cafeteria. They always keep their desks neat and orderly, as if anticipating an inspection. Even their conversation voice contains excess decibels. Now this modus operandi works well when dealing with people who are quite young and less experienced, in a situation when disobeying an order may have dire consequences. In everyday corporate life, however, employees may well have more experience than the manager.

Management-by-order works well when the recipient of such a directive shoulders little or no responsibility for the outcome. Nonetheless, in today's workplace, management tends to share the burden of wrong decisions with employees. How is this done? As a professional employee, your participation in functions that affect anything assumes your compliance. If you do not speak up, then that is your fault. However, by speaking up you will sometimes walk a dangerous path because it's as if you disobeyed a direct order. That act may mean your banishment from the ranks of those labeled "team players," a most desirable label in any large corporation.

The Evasive Manager

Getting a definite yes or no to a specific question is not possible from a dedicated apostle of shifty maneuvers. The evasive manager wants to hedge all bets by couching any reply in vague and mysterious verbosity. A lot of her communication is oral so she can massage any statement to fit a particular future circumstance. She thus appears to emerge a winner in any long-term controversies occurring within the company because over time people's memories cannot compete with selected scripted text. This manager even hedges responses to personal queries, such as an employee's request to take his vacation, by appearing to give an OK but wanting the employee to take responsibility for this consent. She uses phrases and statements like "If your work is on schedule . . ." or "Are all outstanding issues resolved?"

Erma Evasive is a good-natured person who avoids face-to-face confrontations. Why? Because this type of activity often requires succinct communication so that winners and losers can be clearly identified. If drawn into any direct debate, Erma resorts to using her highly honed skill of verboseness to support the illusion that she agrees with an adversary's points—when in fact Erma may be an advocate of the opposite viewpoint. By not appearing to take sides, lines of communication continue to remain open, and personal feelings are not bruised. Erma knows that one of the worst things that can occur in large corporations is to be shut out of what's happening.

Experience demonstrates that when employees operate in the spotlight, their activities become the object of close scrutiny. Therefore, Erma likes to operate behind the scenes to accomplish her job. Whenever promises are made by a behind-the-scenes manager, the details of the commitments are not usually well known. This allows for a degree of flexibility that is not possible in any publicized covenant. Dates, costs, forecasts, and so on can all be massaged to coincide with reality. A manager who operates in this manner usually gains a reputation for being highly reliable. However, this anointment may be completely undeserved. Recognizing this type of maneuver is a gift reserved for the insightful few.

The Manager Who Has a Personality Conflict

One of the main functions of a manager is to motivate employees to perform the required tasks associated with a job. He doesn't do the actual work himself because there is simply too much for one individual to accomplish in a reasonable amount of time. Experience shows that employee stimulation needs to be achieved, while maintaining respect for the individual at all costs. This latter characteristic should be the key ingredient in any manager-employee relationship because it provides a bond that can have a lasting impact. Respect breeds trust, and trust breeds loyalty. The benefits are enormous. However, sometimes respect is discarded in favor of medieval schemes meant to obtain results without regard for people's feelings. It is relatively easy to stimulate an employee to temporarily work harder based on traditional intimidation tactics, which include employment termination threats, low performance rankings, mandatory overtime (usually uncompensated), and ridicule of the employee's accomplishments. It is always an unpleasant experience to become the object of another's caustic behavior. Any manager needs to deliberate on any action that yields a short-term gain at the expense of a permanently scarred employee.

Undoubtedly, the job-hopping opportunities of a professional employee are relatively abundant in the early stages of his career. Young Joe Employee, therefore, doesn't respond to scare tactics used by management. In fact, it infuriates him. Knowing his options, a derided employee may subconsciously resort to a finesse that levels the playing field: Do unto others as they do unto you. The game is for high stakes, and there are really no winners. Although others may view this series of events as open hostility, Joe Employee's thought process easily justifies using the same tactics as those directed at him. He may even resort to visual effects that give the perception of success and power to one-up his adversarial manager. An updated wardrobe, a new car (flashier than his manager's), and a new hairstyle (his manager may be getting bald) all further the desired perception that Joe is superior to his manager. Remarks questioning the ability of those making the decisions endear him to fellow workers. The employee is having fun playing this game. However, the end result is a reciprocal antagonism that soon escalates into a wide-open personality conflict.

Unfortunately, such occurrences are more common than people care to admit. Recognize the symptoms (mutual fault picking regarding physical, mental, behavioral, and attitude characteristics). Cut your losses as soon as possible by distancing yourself from this unpleasant atmosphere. Get another job. It is quite difficult for the manager to acknowledge such a happening because an admission would mean a people-handling failure occurred under his supervision.

If it becomes known that a manager is having or has had a personality conflict with one of his employees, then dire career repercussions occur for the manager. It doesn't even matter if the disharmony was originally the fault of the employee. The fact remains that the manager was a participant in a tactic that is an anathema in the administrative world. No thinking individual will want to work for a person whose disposition interferes with the work experience. Any such manager should eventually be removed from the ranks of administrators and persuaded to seek employment elsewhere.

The Upwardly Mobile Manager

A main objective of a department manager should be to motivate subordinates so the company realizes a maximum return from their work efforts. However, there exists a class of administrators who think the employees exist to further their individual management careers. In large companies this is more prevalent than one would expect. Because there exist layers and layers of management staffing, the primary evidence of success is to become a manager, then a manager of managers, then a manager of managers who manage managers, and so on. It seems as if upwardly mobile people start lobbying for their next promotion on the first day in their newly obtained positions.

Some managers do accomplish individual recognition through hard work. They perform their assigned tasks on time, and the resultant products meet most if not all expectations. Sometimes requirements might even be exceeded. They accomplish all this activity while maintaining the respect of those responsible for actually doing the work. A promotion may then result. This is how the company advertises successful management employees. Sadly, there are other methods that work equally well. One such method is the upwardly mobile manager method. This kind of management style is mostly apparent in large organizations. (Smaller companies couldn't afford such happenings because everyone needs to contribute.) The primary focus of the upwardly mobile managers is pleasing the management above them in the corporate hierarchy chain. They somehow feel the mundane efforts associated with actually performing assigned responsibilities will happen without any significant guidance from them.

So what do these people do to occupy their time? As you might expect, they become excellent pitchmen. They always have a set of charts/foils that tells a story about how successfully their job responsibilities are progressing. In the beginning they concentrate on telling their narratives to the management immediately above them. Then this deftness eventually progresses to include any other higher-level manager willing to listen. Taking numerous trips out of town to other physical locations is one sure sign that things are going according to plan. Eventually, corporate headquarters is sure to be included on the travel itinerary. All this effort gives the appearance of immense involvement and dedication to everyone except those in the department(s) under the upwardly mobile manager's control. What is disturbing is that these managers use people in their organizations to contribute to their own career ambitions by having these people make charts, brief them, answer questions asked by the managers' superiors, and so on. All the while, such diverted employees are not able to contribute to the work at hand, and any respect they had for their managers evaporates. Ironically, upwardly mobile managers are the most eligible to be promoted because they are not needed in their present job assignments.

Interestingly, upwardly mobile managers eventually become so adept at this game that they manipulate their superiors in a similar fashion as they do their direct employees. This leads to a variation of this ruse known as *the managers who manage upward.*

The Risk-Taking Manager

Individuals who take risks need not be adventurous, possess above-average intelligence, or have visionary thoughts. Risk takers are often ordinary Joes who feel comfortable living on the edge. Some of this demeanor comes from not knowing exactly what they are getting into. Perhaps if managers did their homework and understood the success/failure probabilities, they would not be so eager to take a big gamble. Risk categories include schedules, quality, technical feasibility, and employee skill shortages. Some of the characteristics and behavioral traits of these people are as follows:

- ⬧ They commit to situations and conditions that are unrealistic. This is not as dangerous as it might seem because, in large corporations, experience teaches that it is first necessary to acquire responsibility for a project and then figure out how to do it. The savvy manager knows conditions change, and she is a master at manipulating reality to suit her needs.
- ⬧ They minimize any negatives and focus on everything working out in the end. A risk taker never dwells on failure. She relies on

others to perform the checks-and-balances function. (Actually this optimistic outlook is very necessary because if a feeling of "I may not be able to do it" creeps into a risk taker's mental state, then she probably won't do it. She has to believe to succeed.)

↩ They go for broke rather than plan for incremental breakthroughs.

↩ Their delivery schedules assume excessive amounts of overtime.

↩ They may have nothing to lose because they may already be "on the ropes." An unexpected success can boost any sagging career. Besides, this type of manager can always claim the reason for a job loss was that their gamble didn't pan out. It doesn't sound as bad as being bounced for incompetence.

↩ They sometimes rely on the fact that they will not have to directly follow through on the shaky venture. The risk can be delegated to other unsuspecting employees.

↩ Seasoned risk takers know that high-risk endeavors seldom have to succeed. In fact large companies like to popularize the notion that a failed endeavor will probably not adversely affect a person's career. In any event such managers gain notoriety for their daring actions.

Most real risks involve crisis, and a real crisis breeds solutions, which normally take long periods of time to construct and carry out. Most companies are willing to deviate from normal practice to support an uncertain endeavor that has the approval of high level management. Meanwhile, the imagined champion (Human Resources) of the employee may busy itself with reminding managers of potential labor-law violations rather than taking any action to ensure the physical and mental well-being of overworked employees putting in, say, 100 plus hours per week. In short, an employee's private life is sometimes put on hold to support risky projects. Other procedures that are normally in place to ensure things like quality can also be compromised in order to assist shaky ventures.

The Manager Who Keeps Employees on the Hook

Some managers resort to a maneuver known as *keeping employees on the hook*. Its execution is quite simple. A manager puts people on the defensive by continually giving them assignments without waiting for the completion of prior tasks. Now, some in the management game view this as acceptable behavior. They justify this conduct under the mask of productivity. Managers need to appreciate the fact that piling up assignments for an employee without recognizing that employee's intervening successes can demoralize the most conscientious worker. Even government guidelines suggest a break from continuous workdays. Everyone needs some respite from a heavy workload. College students take a summer pause from the grind of doing homework day after day. Besides, college students can realize accomplishment regularly by scoring well on tests. Tests offer a cleansing opportunity to unload the burden of accumulated knowledge and start fresh on another learning adventure. Working for a corporation should offer the same benefits in this regard.

Too often, lengthy on-the-hook stints result in early employee burnout. The company loses because the employee attitude becomes one of simply working for a paycheck. Employees' initiative disappears because any suggestion they offer will probably add to their backlog of things to do. Burnout leads to turnover, and turnover contributes to lower-quality products and services. Still, some managers are so myopic that they cannot see beyond the next deadline.

Additionally, if an administrator's style is dominated by on-the-hook characteristics, this allows him to hide his incompetence from others. It gives him freedom to pursue other things, like attending meetings to occupy his time. There is no time for him to discuss. There is only time to delegate.

The Manager Who Remains on the Periphery

Non-management employees who operate on the sidelines court the risk of becoming a non-essential ingredient of their department's function. However, often this condition happens through no fault of their own. So, as a working employee, be on the lookout for the most prevalent periphery symptom: drifting into a state of non-communication. In the same way, even if a manager disagrees with the department's goals or the means of accomplishing such goals, she needs to stay involved to effect change. Otherwise that person loses any influence she may have possessed because she is out of touch with what's happening. She is unable to make any meaningful contribution.

But contrary to logical reasoning, when the sideline employee happens to be a manager, benefits may sometimes accrue while she is operating in this mode. Administrators delight in projecting the image that their non-involvement is a sign of superior managerial skills. The thinking goes something like this: Because a department's commitments are continually satisfied in a timely manner with acceptable or even superior quality, the manager must have done a good job in the following areas:

> ⟜ Delegating authority
> ⟜ Assigning the right people to the right tasks
> ⟜ Putting the proper procedures in place

In reality, the cause for success is most likely because of the quality of the manager's employees or just dumb luck.

Because a sideline manager needs something to occupy her workdays, she will likely attend meetings that offer the necessary exposure required for her to advance up the company promotion ladder. An overly ambitious person may even accept assignments at such gatherings to cultivate the illusion that she is ready for more formidable tasks. This is an aggressive tactic because sideline players usually isolate themselves from being associated with anything that could misfire. That's why they chose to be peripheral players in the first place. Because some uncertainty is involved here, careful selection of a low-risk assignment is critical. Telling others about its pumped-up difficulty always helps in the perception game. Therefore, a manager can manipulate her state of being a peripheral player to convey the impression that she is doing an excellent job in her present job slot and is thus available for an advancement.

Conversely, managers who are busy and involved are not looked upon favorably for several reasons. First, they are unknown. They have no time for the exposure game, the perception game, and the managing-upward game. Second, those in charge perceive that they obviously have not done the proper job of managing because their presence seems critical to the success of assigned departmental tasks. Justifying a promotion for an individual based on involvement and work ethic is somewhat difficult. She is a critical component in her present assignment. She is therefore not mobile. Twisted thinking? It happens every day.

The Confrontational Manager

Ever meet an individual who engages in conversation by challenging everything people say? Well, some managers control employees in this manner. It gives them a feeling of authority even though they may know nothing about the subject under discussion. The theory here is that employees properly intimidated will work harder. Unfortunately, needless confrontations consume time and result in workers mentally preparing responses for conflicts that may never occur. Eventually such a manager is ignored by others. Respect, trust, and loyalty soon disappear from the forced manager-employee relationship. Nobody enjoys being on constant alert or being put on the defensive.

The Manager Who Doesn't Want to Be a Manager

Occasionally an individual is drafted to become the department manager to fill an immediate need. Rapid expansion, promotional opportunity, illness of the former manager, and so on can create this situation (real or imagined). The allure of attaining management status may be too much for the manager-elect to turn down. The only thing certain in the mystic world of people administration is he will get to include the experience on his resume. Most draftees accept the assignment as a temporary career detour. But accomplishment is often an elusive objective once an individual accepts the role of a "people pusher."

At first, the conscript manager may even *enjoy* the perks that accompany the role of administrator. A private office with a view, memo correspondence for managers' eyes only, access to personnel jackets of fellow employees, and meetings that elevate his skill at gamesmanship all can contribute to the perceived joy of becoming a manager. Then stark reality may creep back into life at work: Logic can sometimes be a hindrance. A simple example illustrates this point. Let's say the draftee is told by his manager to direct individuals in his department to work overtime (unpaid most likely), which is clearly unnecessary. He convinces himself that this is one of those abstract management techniques that is supposed to create a feeling of solidarity and urgency among the troops. Officially, upper management declares that the extra hours are needed to maintain focus. However, thinking people quickly reject maneuvers such as forced togetherness and a false state of crisis. Such tactics contribute to the continued loss of respect for a management more adept at mind games than facing reality. Nonetheless, the draftee's balking at such a directive would be interpreted as not being part of the team. So unpleasant task No. 1 gets executed.

Time goes by, and the manager (who didn't want to be) feels his principles are slowly eroding. What to do? Well, the resume objective is satisfied, so one tested method of extracting one's self from an unpleasant job situation is to create an "incident." This deed needs to be implemented in a manner that can succeed independent of whether upper management agrees or disagrees with the motive. For example, the unhappy manager may write a memo indicating his willingness to take responsibility for a committed technical assignment of dubious success. The copy list contains the right people to ensure that his immediate management cannot ignore such a move. (This element is the key ingredient that guarantees success.) Others look upon this act as volunteering for failure. However, they forget the conscript is not a career manager but a skilled employee.

The strategy works, and the defrocked employee is reassigned. Unfortunately, he is banished to an obscure office. This exile is deemed necessary as a visual warning to others who may be so inclined. Management doesn't like to be coerced into people moves it did not originate. The company handles the resulting administrative vacancy by simply assigning this function to another person who may already be responsible for two departments. The change occurs without a ripple in any departmental commitments. Looks like the original need for a new manager was imaginary.

The delighted ex-manager is now free to do the things he enjoys without the distraction of playing the management game. Once again, he looks forward to coming to work.

Pitfalls of the Manager's Manual

Only corporate-approved rules are supplied in the manager's manual. These rules are meant to cover most employee-management situations. The company's explanation for having such a document is that it is necessary to maintain a degree of uniformity in the treatment of its employees. However, seasoned workers know that the hidden intent of such a manual is to guarantee that the company's official position on any topic ends up on the right side of any government-endorsed labor law.

Often administrators consult the Human Resources (HR) Department to interpret the rules in the manager's manual. The translation seldom favors the employee. However, the company may go to great lengths to publicize those token rulings, painting itself as the benevolent corporate employer. Remember that the imagined impartiality of HR is always tainted by the conflict of interest that pits *serving the management in power* against *objective reasoning.*

To its credit the company realizes that it is impossible to state a rule for every situation, so it grants some leeway to its management in the handling of extraordinary situations. Yet this freedom can cause employee confusion because identical circumstances may be handled in contradictory ways, depending on whom one's manager happens to be at the time. Whenever this difference is brought to the attention of the HR Department, the HR staff may ignore the inconsistency or invoke its obfuscation facade delivered with a smile and a handshake. A position of *always supporting the management in power* can lead to incompatible and irrational behavior.

What Makes a Good Manager

People become managers for many reasons, but few succeed at this job. This is partially because holding a position in management is different than being a productive worker. Too often a new manager will continue to do her former job without motivating others to do theirs. She may end up working long hours trying to perform two functions and fail miserably at the people aspect of management. The manager may end up competing with her own employees, and the workers may resent it immensely. Rather, a good manager should do the following things:

- Act as a buffer between her employees and the outside distractions occurring both within and outside the company. Her department's productivity will suffer if she doesn't filter all the unnecessary rhetoric that hits her desk.
- Express her displeasure as a rational being against illogical company policies, strategy, and so on. She will gain the immediate respect of her employees. Remember that a company is not the military, where people blindly follow orders.
- Act as a caring individual who understands that people have lives outside of work. She should realize that asking people to work overtime is disruptive and can cause additional stress.
- Defend her workers against all attacks made by competing departments.
- Never attempt to scam an employee into believing something the employee knows to be false (for example, by giving an invalid explanation of why an expected raise was not given or a bogus reason for a low performance rating, or by upholding the validity of the company's stumbling strategy).
- Never discipline an erring employee in front of his peers. The employee will never forget the humiliating experience, and the manager will lose the confidence of her workers because they will believe that "open season" can be declared on anyone in the department.
- Act as a model for others to emulate. This includes dress, mannerisms, and ethics. Earlier it was stated that people tend to imitate the so-called movers and shakers (this can include both good and bad people) in a company. On the negative side, this imitation can surface as anything from using gutter English in meetings to impress the timid to distorting facts in order to gain

an upper hand in a technical confrontation. Remember that, sooner or later, the obnoxious people will either move on to something else or be removed from a management position after their work habits are exposed. Workers never forget the transparency of wannabes that pander to obnoxious people, hoping to gain favor in the short term.

↭ Share credit with members of the department when she is recognized as the manager of the group that did an outstanding job. Demonstrating one's bigness is often more rewarding than receiving personal accolades for a job well done.

↭ Help in the career advancement of workers in her department. Soon others will recognize that she is the manager to work for, and she will be deluged with people wanting to be in her department. This attribute helps the manager too because she gets to choose from a larger list of qualified workers and indirectly her status increases for bringing out the best in each employee.

↭ Walk the aisles for visibility with the people who do the work. Some managers wrongly believe they can manage from behind a desk.

In summary, good managerial skills focus on the intangibles that cause others to produce superior products/services. This can range from the constant refinement of the processes by which products/services are produced, marketed, and serviced to the motivation of workers so they can attain their full potential. This is the positive side that managers should always present to the work force. Even an incompetent employee would appreciate a manager who needs to fire him but says it in a positive and honest way ("Your verbal communication skills indicate that you should be employed in a job that utilizes those talents.") instead of a crude way ("You talk too much. Therefore I need to let you go.").

What Makes a Bad Manager

Bad managers have a way of creeping into positions of power by disguising their true reasons for accepting such a job. These reasons may include anything from removing themselves from the daily task of producing real work that they cannot do well to believing that it is easier to direct, monitor, follow, track, suggest, and verbalize than to produce. People who slide into management with these attributes almost always resort to the political aspects of being managers. This is not to say that some skill in politics is not required to be a good manager, but people can use the mask of politics to guarantee that they are never held responsible for anything. Bad managers typically do the following things:

- Shift the blame to other members of the department when something goes wrong. This can vary from missing a commitment to expressing their displeasure about the lack of team effort. Remember that if anyone is responsible for building the team, it is the manager.

- Avoid confrontation with an employee who is obviously disrupting the work of others because the managers do not have sufficient confidence in their abilities to correct the situation. This can go on for years, and the situation can deteriorate such that productive employees are forced to leave the department out of frustration and most likely will exit the company for greener pastures.

- Never accept challenging assignments that have a degree of risk because, after all, they get paid whether they produce or not in a big corporation. Managers have been known to hide for years without contributing anything.

- Adhere to standard procedures that may or may not contribute to the success of the assignments given to their departments. Bad managers believe they can always say they followed the guidelines, and this sounds good. They never question whether it makes sense or if it impedes progress.

- Quote others in authority so that if anything goes wrong, they can shed responsibility by pointing to others.

- Carefully attend all the right meetings to visibly show others their loyalty. Never mind if they are not doing real work. They could not care less if a meeting accomplishes nothing. This is particularly true of regular gatherings (say, every week) that meet whether there is anything to discuss or not.

- Hide behind company policy when situations that cause employees stress occur in their departments. This characteristic is especially demeaning when part of the company policy is liberal enough to include a manager discretion clause. For example, if a conscientious worker needs time off to take care of a personal problem, and the manager says that he cannot give time off without deducting money from the worker's paycheck, the company will lose in the long run because of the ill will harbored by the employee. When the time comes for the employee to put forth an extra effort, you can be sure she will remember past treatment.

- ⊷ Cannot evaluate the work done by their employees, so they use such mundane indicators as time spent on the job rather than what was actually produced.
- ⊷ Continually tout company slogans, such as producing products that are "world class," are "ISO 9000 compliant," and have "zero defects." This propaganda sounds good to the uninformed, but constantly feeding it to employees only weakens the intended effect.

In the face of the previous points, which expose the realities of working in a large corporation, there will most likely be an outcry from people who consider themselves competent managers. These people see themselves as the real decision makers in the organization when actually only the top few rate that description. The fact is that most managers perform repetitive chores far removed from producing something that makes the company money.

Some Accoutrements and Mannerisms of Large-Company Management

When an individual becomes a manager, he sometimes undergoes a metamorphosis meant to differentiate himself from the non-management employees. Both physical and psychological changes can occur. The office space of a manager is often bigger, better decorated, and more strategically located than those of his direct employees. A bigger desk and chair may make him seem more powerful, while smaller chairs are reserved for employees. This physical difference can give a mental edge to the manager and help sell the viewpoints of management in confrontational situations. Time and talent are not always needed to make an unpopular decision accepted. He may hang plaques on his office wall to attest to the training he has received in company-sponsored classes. This somehow makes his position more official and is intended to strengthen the perception of wisdom and impartiality.

The work habits and mannerisms of managers are meant to foster the notion of stability, loyalty, and—above all—well-thought-out plans and direction. Sometimes it seems as if a management career has been elevated to a true science. However, experience demonstrates that the administration of people is more of an art because it deals with individuals who have feelings and need motivation. Good management is highly dependent on individual personalities. Nevertheless, large companies tend to think managers should be interchangeable so no one becomes indispensable. To conform to the management image a corporation wants, administrators tend to isolate themselves from their employees. They go to lunch together, dress more formally, have similar outside interests, and above all promote the company line—even if, inside, they know it to be in error. However, this differentiation of external appearance contributes to the gap that often exists between management and its workers. But remember that in today's professional ranks, the real workers are just as educated as the people who manage them.

On investigation it becomes apparent that new, dynamic companies do not possess such attitudes regarding a conforming management. They concentrate on the job at hand and resort to most anything to achieve their goals. If an employee needs a bigger office to accommodate her library reference material, then an office exchange may occur, which then reinforces the bond between a manager and his employees. Such occurrences are nearly impossible in a large corporation. This is one reason why new companies are so successful even when they compete against companies much larger, with more resources, and more experience.

Management's Global Judgment of Employees' Contributions

How do corporations measure the productivity of professional workers? Most apply yardsticks that are easy to understand but that unfortunately usually apply to other activities, such as manufacturing. For example, in software development, productivity is usually measured in lines of code per unit of time. What management misses is that inefficient code results in more lines of code than efficient code. So the effect is to reward people who make inferior products. Ironic but true. Standards for productivity also often miss the point that products created with unrealistic schedules usually result in defects that would not have occurred if reasonable time had been allotted to do the job right. Other tactics upon which management relies to judge employees' everyday efforts include the following:

> ✧ Frequently, workers are judged by the number of hours they work rather than the work produced. This makes it easy for workers to be evaluated by management because it seems that the individual with the greatest number of hours per unit of time will naturally

turn out to be the best employee. This removes any requirement for a management analysis to determine the real value of individual employees.

⮞ Instead of realizing that if a selected process works for a particular individual then it is OK for that person to use, management often wants to define a process that applies to all. The amount of time corporations spend on this process activity is unbelievable. Meanwhile enlightened companies are laughing all the way to introducing new and exciting products/services. Ask yourself this: If a cure for the common cold was not discovered by an approved corporate process standard for research, would people buy it? Of course they would, unencumbered with the knowledge that it did not conform to Corporation X's method for doing research.

The Information Gap

An information gap always seems to exist between what management knows and what it shares with the working staff. Granted, some news is properly reserved only for managers (for example, candidates for layoff). However, withholding information indiscriminately causes a lack of trust and unnecessary friction. Too often, this repression of knowledge becomes a habit. Some managers seem to take joy in the fact that they know something their workers don't. Sounds like a game suited for pre-teen children.

Pay grids are a good example of information hiding in some companies. What reason exists to prohibit employees access to the compensation received at all levels within their job classifications? What risk is involved? In fact having these data might offer an incentive for superior performance. Some administrators justify this repression activity by saying, "Non-managers may not be able to handle bad news" or "Filtered knowledge is better than no knowledge." These views further promote the notion that somehow the company believes that lower-level workers are less mature, less educated, less motivated, or less loyal.

Now consider the state of the company's business if employees withheld information from their department managers. Schedules would be missed, problems would never surface, and chaos would reign. Employees would be chastised for their unwillingness to communicate. Managers would be helpless because their jobs depend on good communication.

They would most likely fail. The absurdity of this situation would not be tolerated. So why is the reverse application sanctioned?

Some Dangers of Withholding Information

Even if the official position of the company prohibits the dissemination of "anticipated" information beyond management ranks, leaks do occur. Any leak may be stroked, extrapolated, or abbreviated along its way to anxious listeners. This unofficial information can cause other related hearsay to surface. Pretty soon, information that was privileged may spawn a whole series of rumors whose credibility was boosted by some half-truths contained in leaked knowledge. This leads to difficulties for management, which now needs to deal with large doses of massaged information.

Of course, sophisticated employees have come to appreciate the difference between intentional and unintentional leaks. A deliberate leak can affect the duration of pleasant news. For example, an unexpected rise in company earnings may be discussed at length before official information is released for public consumption.

The Big Boys from Corporate

On occasion the management team from the corporate offices visits company-wide sites to get a bird's-eye view of what's happening. In theory it sounds like an opportunity for upper-level managers to understand things at the worker level, but the realities often suggest otherwise. Local management usually prepares for this event like it is a rare opportunity to make a lot of points with the big boys. Productive work may effectively stop, with real work being put on the shelf so workers can prepare presentations and demonstrations for the visiting bigwigs. Most of the time, it doesn't even matter if the boys from corporate are treated to a dog-and-pony show. It's the perception that counts. Ask any manager. (You would think the corporate boys would be more savvy about such things because many of them probably did it themselves on the way to headquarters.) So misinformation may flourish as local management presents continued optimism about product quality, progress, commitments, and so on. The objective seems to be to withhold any bad news because this can be revealed later, preferably remotely by telephone on Friday at 5 p.m. Whenever the corporate boys visit with the real workers, they are usually carefully led to individuals who have been prepped about what to say and how to act. The behavior of such selected individuals often borders on paying homage to a head of state.

At corporate headquarters, the illusion game may be played in earnest. From the suits they wear to the mannerisms that rub off on the wannabes, life in the perception lane is often full of insecure people hoping to give the impression that they are all-American boys who serve the interests of the company at all costs. Lack of experience never slows down these driven individuals. Most of them believe in the axiom, "Ambition provides ability." Attendance at meeting after meeting often feeds the egos of the boys at corporate. The names given to some of these meetings may borrow heavily from the military world to instill a sense of urgency. The words, *task force, strategic,* and *tactical* have all been used to give the perception of national importance.

Late night phone calls from corporate headquarters to work sites in different time zones may further the perception that the big boys burn the candle as dedicated employees. They are usually not discussing work items on the phone but just extending an impression that they care about what the local managers are doing. Soon the remote-site managers may catch on to this game and start their workdays later and later so that when the late night phone calls start coming in, they are there. The local boys still only are at work eight hours per day but give the illusion that they are working overtime. The cycle is self-perpetuating, and soon the "workaholics" at the production site may be promoted to corporate headquarters because of the effort they put into the job of game playing.

Titled Management and Its Hidden Faults

Just like the military, corporations have developed a series of titles to enhance the perceived importance of people's positions. These titles are sometimes even used to assuage the egos of individuals in lieu of monetary benefits. Along with titles come other perks, such as the size of one's office, its decorations, its view, and its proximity to offices of higher levels of management. Obtaining a respected title is like becoming a member of a good-old-boy club because managers with important-sounding titles tend to take care of their own. For example, when a position opens up because of a reorganization, titled managers usually end up on their feet. This practice ensures continued allegiance from the titled manager, thus enforcing the power of the club. It also demonstrates to others that being a member of the good-old-boy team pays off.

Titles both inside and outside the corporation (witness the number of bank vice presidents) can dazzle the unknowing. However, it is often difficult to detect the true nature of one's job assignment based on the title alone. The title of director is especially nebulous because directing some activity can range from being responsible for managing a group of landscape workers to being a member of the board of directors for a company. The titles of chairperson, president, vice president, general manager, director, and functional manager all possess an abstractness that can give the titles' present occupants a mystique of being all-knowing and all-powerful. In fact the same title in different companies and even in different divisions within the same company can have entirely different duties. Some titled managers are fond of stating that they do whatever the job requires. However, many are free to define the job requirements as they see them, so who can measure their performance?

In reality, most titled managers depend on others to keep them informed of what's going on, and they rarely mingle with the actual workers. Most titled managers have forgotten how to communicate with the individuals who do the real work and thus surround themselves with people who are assigned this task. Unfortunately, such subordinates tend to water down unpleasant facts because of the kill-the-messenger syndrome that has survived from ancient times and continues to persist in modern organizations.

Executive Paths to Wealth

The people who direct the fortunes of large companies usually receive compensation packages that far outweigh their contributions to the company coffers. Especially in times of financial distress, deals are often struck in panic to rescue the company. Such deals may assure the wily executive that she will receive an outrageous income for the rest of her life, no matter if the company succeeds or fails in the marketplace. Consequently, some executives have caught on to the notion that it is far better to work on a contract basis rather than work as a regular employee. By doing this, they negotiate for stock options, buyouts (in case they are dumped for whatever reason), deferred compensation, and the like. The contracts are legally enforceable, so unlike the dedicated thirty-year employee who receives a paltry sum of money (if any) when he is terminated by a layoff, fired for incompetence, or induced to leave because of age, high-level terminated executives usually reap a windfall of income. In fact in some cases it seems better to be relieved of a position as a company executive rather than to continue working.

In addition, company compensation committees (a group decision shares the blame if anything goes wrong) may make it a point to say that in order to remain competitive with executive pay in other organizations, they must pay executives up to several hundred times what their regular factory workers make—despite the fact that scores of qualified candidates within their own company could probably do the job at least as well as the person who is being courted to take over the company fortunes. In a lot of cases, the sought-after executive has absolutely no experience in the line of business she is being asked to lead. This is because some executives who define the rules of the business game believe the precept that once someone is a manager, she can manage anything. Can you translate this line of reasoning to the case of an engineering manager who is laid off and then applies for a job as a manager of physicians at a hospital? Of course not.

What outside candidates may have that other qualified candidates lack is a reputation for increasing a company's profitability. Unfortunately, they usually accomplish this simply by shedding employees while claiming that only deadwood and non-essential business areas will be affected. In the short term, this almost always works, but such an executive is usually keenly aware that she should be looking for other opportunities before it becomes apparent that no long-term strategy for growing the business exists. Ironically, if she lands a new job, the new company must compensate the raided company for early termination of her agreement. If she has no luck in securing other employment, she may be comforted by the fact that when she is finally recognized as ineffective, her employment contract will make her a very rich individual.

However, if the company begins to show profitability, the next step such executives can use to increase the return of the financial package contracted at their hiring is to influence buying back the company's stock on the open market. They usually do this to publicly demonstrate the financial health of the company. On the surface, this act shows confidence in their leadership while at the same time creating an artificial demand for the stock. To nobody's surprise, the price of the stock rises. Why do this? Simply put, it increases the value of *their* stock options. This may be a subconscious happening, but its effect is the same. The current stockholders often lose sight of this ploy because their holdings appear to be worth more. When the company buying cannot be sustained, reality returns to the stock market, but by this time the executive has most likely exercised her options and unloaded them. It's neat, quick, and legal, and nobody gets hurt—except the inexperienced public.

Executives also have other avenues to wealth through companies by which they are not directly employed. For example, company directors who are not employees of that company receive significant annual retainers, plus additional fees for chairing board committees, plus an additional fee for each meeting attended. Travel, lodging, and other expenses related to board meetings are also reimbursable. Life and health insurance benefits in addition to stock options are also usually a part of a director's compensation package. Gaining membership on boards of various companies can be like collecting trophies in the business world. Imagine being a board member of five or ten companies. Really, how much can such overextended people contribute to the running of any business? Additionally, it seems as if board membership is a perquisite reserved for the good-old-boy network. Usually directors are friends of the people who appoint them, and so instead of being unbiased watchdogs, they often function in the interests of those who appointed them. And the money machine usually doesn't stop when they are no longer active members of the board. In retirement they often receive annual compensation that may equal their yearly retainer with as little service as five to ten years. All this for optionally attending a couple of meetings a year?

The Management Two-step, As Applied to Employee Evaluation

Managers are supposed to really shine when it comes to evaluating employees and their accompanying contributions to the company business. Good managers surround themselves with competent individuals. When employees succeed, so too does management. This association fosters victory for all. Some managers even boast that they can evaluate someone in a first encounter of five to ten minutes. Unfortunately, variables such as a favor owed, mannerisms, and background information all can play a role in arriving at a final employee assessment. And many managers think it is always appropriate to adopt any new evaluation gimmick that comes along, making the company appear leading-edge.

The 360° evaluation method (note that this is supposed to be all-encompassing, like 360° in a circle) is a prime example of the something-new-so-it-must-be-better phenomenon. Give something a catchy tag, and it often immediately becomes the latest and greatest. Proponents of 360° evaluation hope to gain notoriety by popularizing this responsibility-avoiding maneuver throughout the corporate fraternity. Through this evaluation method, managers will no longer have total responsibility in evaluating their employees. It gets to be formally shared with others. As implemented in some companies, the 360° evaluation technique allows each employee to select a number of fellow employees to give their appraisals of the first employee's contributions during a period of time. What usually happens is that employees only select people who will give favorable input. Some management proponents argue, however, that they always asked for input from others when assessing an employee's performance. The difference 360° evaluation interjects is that the employee gets to select the evaluation team. How could anyone get a low score using this technique? Another objective of 360° evaluation is to make employees feel that they now have a greater say in what's going on. However, some employees think it's just another game that takes time away from doing anything useful.

Why do these new people-management gimmicks keep surfacing in the corporate world? Well, it seems as if today's corporations want to remove subjectivity and replace it with objectivity when dealing with the people resource. Treating individuals as objects suggests employees are just a part of the community of inanimate commodities. Using the term *Human Resource Department* as opposed to *Personnel Department* has reinforced the notion of the people commodity. Like new math, all the "in" phrases and practices will disappear when companies discover that they negatively affect the bottom-line profit objective.

Management Tainted by Inbreeding

In most big companies, the policy to fill open management slots is to limit the selection process to candidates already employed within the organization. On rare occasions a nominee is brought in from outside the current structure (but still employed by the same company), and still rarer is the case of an aspirant from another company entirely. If either of the latter two cases occurs, this is most likely because the open position is in deep trouble. The locals were probably already polled, and no one wanted the job. So be careful if you are ever offered a low- to medium-level management position by a corporation other than your current employer. In contrast, high-level management slots may carry a lot of baggage and associated risk, but applicants for these slots usually know how to negotiate a parachute deal before accepting employment. Contractual agreements are more common than most employees realize. It's interesting to observe that the higher that people advance in a corporation, the more they seem to become suspicious of their tenure.

To the casual observer, picking a manager from within seems the right thing to do. It is widely believed that doing so will positively affect employees' morale. However, some unpleasant side effects need to be exposed. The tendency is to promote individuals who possess a similar background to those already in management. Although this can be successful for a time, the practice invites inbreeding of conventional thought, communication, and behavior. In such a situation, it becomes difficult to differentiate one manager from the other. Employees can eventually predict any manager's response to a particular stimulus with a large degree of success. Memos rely on the same buzzword phrases, as this verbiage permeates all communication. Inbred managers often even emulate one another's mannerisms, such as lighting a cigarette using certain hand movements, answering a question with a question, and participating in conversations with an intermittent "hmm," which may imply concurrence, opposition, or whatever seems to fit the particular situation.

In times of company prosperity, corporate dogma supports the notion that the conforming of thought processes by people in management is actually a good thing. It seems that only in times of crisis does management tolerate conflicting beliefs. Never forget that there is a continuing need to question, critique, and disagree because conformity becomes a breeding ground for complacency. The close cousins of apathy, indifference, and self-absorption become an accepted way of life for managers who do things because they feel an extreme need to belong. Similar peer managers make life comfortable, while unlike peers can make people think.

Surviving Employee Confrontations with Management

From time to time, an employee must interact with the management of the company for a variety of reasons. These may include addressing topics such as compensatory time off for unpaid overtime worked, a vacation that is interrupted because of a perceived problem that only that employee can solve, and even the eligibility of dependents for certain company benefits. In these and other situations, remember that managers must first look to protect the company. And don't be surprised if they deal with your case by placing the burden of proof directly on you. In any confrontation, understand that management is backed by the Human Resources Department, the Legal Department, line management, the Benefits Department, and so on. With this in mind, do your homework so you understand your rights better than your manager and his supporting cast.

By all means, never confront management without knowing the game rules as well as your adversaries do. Read all the literature (company and otherwise) that is available on the subject. By doing this, you will be equipped—especially if your adversaries assume you know little and try to confuse your case with rhetoric that sounds good but that on closer inspection is proven to be a standard response hoping to derail your situation. Whatever happens, don't despair. Press onward if you believe your case is in the right.

Unfortunately, time is on the side of the corporation. For example, if you believe the company has treated you unjustly, you must take action within a specified time period; otherwise your claim may be denied because the statute of limitations can invalidate it. Even the legal system of our government backs this one up. In such a situation, you may be told that conditions have changed and the individuals responsible for your injustice are no longer performing that function, have transferred to another location, or have even left the company. If this happens, you should remind their successors that these people did not represent themselves but represented the views and policies of the company backed by all the company's resources (for example, legal). The company can sustain its position for a long time hoping that you will be dealing from a position of decreasing vigor. It counts on the advantage of time to weaken its detractors. What if the company tells you that you are right and will be fairly treated? Proceed with caution: This could be a ploy meant to disarm you so that you begin to think well of the company. Look at this tactic carefully, and you may find that the company may never admit wrongdoing. Others in management may even support you, and you may even feel as if you won. But remember that without a final resolution, words and feelings mean nothing.

Management and Multi-location Corporations

Companies that have become quite large tend to have multiple locations across the United States and even the entire world. This encourages the perception of fantastic success and worldwide acceptance of its products. This structure lends itself to a management technique that involves transferring projects in trouble to various locations, as pieces on a chessboard. This feeds the travel egos of some managers because they have less work to do, they can build up their frequent traveler points, and they can make contacts for potential job-enhancement moves. In any case, management from the transferring location usually comes out the winner because if anything goes right it is because the transferring location did such a good job in design, planning, or whatever. However, if anything goes wrong with the project, failure is usually attributed to the receiving location.

When Location X is given a specific mission with firm customer delivery dates, its management may be led to believe that the workers have already absorbed the technical depth that has taken years for the relinquishing site(s) to obtain—so product development may begin on a shaky note. Terms and phrases such as *proactive, technical opportunities, rev it up a notch, risk taking,* and *challenging assignments* may be intended to make up for the lack of management skills in coping with both immediate and strategic problems. By endorsing such catchy phrases, corporations shift accountability (and potential blame if the project fails) to nonmanagers who are usually unaware of what is happening because they are absorbed in trying to meet schedules that they had no say in determining.

Another particularly useful technique available to multi-location corporate management is that employees at locations in unfavorable climates north of the Mason-Dixon line tend to work longer and harder simply because in the winter time, the buildings are heated and properly lit. Employees in warmer climates have a lot of outside activities available to them, relegating work to a lower status. Therefore, workers in these colder climates usually are more productive, have less absenteeism, are more loyal, and work longer hours. However, rather than rewarding cold-climate employees for their diligence, management often tries to convince them that they are lucky to have such good jobs. After all, management may point out, the population shift is to warmer climates, so there are fewer good jobs available in the colder parts of the country. The message is, "Be thankful you have a job."

Some Management Options for Dealing with a "Problem" Employee

Employees who are not performing at an acceptable level are always candidates for dismissal. However, there always seems to be more nominees for such a designation in times of a business downturn. How does management cope? Experience teaches that those in control are free to change the criteria of what constitutes an undesirable employee any time they wish. Tardiness, attendance, dress, and other such things can suddenly take on huge importance. The fact that you continue to do your assignments on time with acceptable quality can be easily discounted.

The process of firing a professional person usually consumes a lot of effort and can last many months. This is because the employee's department manager has to build a case showing that a particular individual is incompetent, has a bad attitude, is negatively influencing others, has committed some transgression, or whatever. A documentation trail must validate the ultimate decision to let someone go. All this behind-the-scenes activity must occur before Human Resources will agree that the required homework has been done. Why is all this formality necessary? Simple: Human Resources' duties include maintaining a semblance of peace, tranquility, and order and, above all, avoiding any possible confrontation with government employment regulations. Therefore, firing someone is looked upon as an undesirable part of doing business. However, management has found other avenues to get rid of "problem" employees.

The most common technique used in dealing with a questionable employee is to transfer her to someone else's department. This procedure is usually quick and bypasses most manager-worker confrontations. If the receiving department has many open head-count requisitions, then this maneuver is accomplished without much work. However, if the targeted department has only a single opening, then the finesse requires persuasive communicative skills. The receiving manager needs to believe that the eligible employee would be an asset to his department. Unfortunately, some managers neglect to ask the opinions of workers who could contribute some insight into this matter. Ego has a way of interfering with common sense, especially in matters of personnel judgment. Management-initiated transfers occur more frequently than anyone might suspect. Euphemistic phrases like *workload balancing* are invoked to conceal any hint that all is not going according to plan.

Another technique often used to ease an undesirable out of a department is to disguise this action as an *opportunity*. Prestigious corporate education classes have been used as a lure to remove an individual from her workplace for one, two, or even three months. Upon return, she may find that her temporarily vacant position has been abolished, and it now may become her own responsibility to find another job within the corporation. This tactic can be particularly successful whenever the employee does not do well in the company-sponsored school.

Turning a Bad Situation into an Opportunity, Manager-Style

Project failure is a fact of life in a big company. However, a pending disaster can also be a career opportunity. Insight and perspective are needed to reveal the full potential of such a situation. The savvy manager understands that taking over a recognized "bad" circumstance is a win-win proposition. He wins if he succeeds in turning a failure into a success.

He still wins if the failure actually happens, because he took the initiative to try and rescue it. Upper management views him as a risk taker, a man of action, a comer.

To fully utilize this situation, it is crucial for others (especially upper management) to understand that the catastrophe is almost guaranteed. Employees usually lose their inhibitions when faced with failure. Truth need not be disguised in euphemistic phrases because job loss is a real possibility. Missed schedules, poor product performance, and less-than-expected function all contribute to the perception of non-success. In short, failure is already presumed, so anything more will be greatly appreciated. An elevation to hero status is more than likely. So taking a chance is not really that dangerous.

Next, the turnaround manager must do his homework. This will most likely reveal the root of the problem. Homework can reveal circumstances as simple as a personality conflict between the leader of the project and its worker staff. Workers almost never buy into something that is associated with their cause of discontent. Think about this for a moment. Having nothing to lose but an unpleasant job does not seem all that bad to workers who are constantly abused by an individual who possesses authority over them but is basically a jerk. The absence of buy-in leads to other ingredients of failure, such as finger pointing and finally a breakdown in communication. When this happens, disaster is certainly assured. Now, it is not unreasonable for employees to expect management to react to their plight. Sometimes, however, this can take a year or more. Often certain people in the management game hesitate, hoping things will somehow work out. A wait-and-see attitude seldom works. Managers are paid to act, not observe. The simple solution, the turnaround manager knows, is to remove the cause of irritation by placing the culpable individual in an advisory position with no real power. This act saves face for management and the defrocked employee. The workers react with a renewed enthusiasm. Problems surface because people begin talking to one another. The insightful turnaround manager may take advantage of this condition by advertising every incremental success. This action further endears him to the reinvigorated worker staff. They work harder. The positive attitude that was absent for so long finally takes hold.

A Look at a Manager Some Years down the Road

What happens to managers after years in the business? Some are elevated to greater positions of responsibility, while a few return to the lower-level ranks. Usually, once people become managers, it is difficult to give it up. They become used to being called managers, their minds have gotten used to concentrating on the big picture, their compensation is better than most if not all of the members of their departments, and they may believe that their jobs are more secure than those of non-managers. Besides, it would be difficult to update their skills to be competitive in the non-manager arena. So most of them stay put rather than risk the uncertainty of change.

Most career managers remain stuck in their original first-line administrative positions. However, first-line managers do lead tough lives. They get flak from their direct department members and their second-line managers. The flak from below comes because employees today speak their minds and can usually find employment elsewhere because they are involved in doing real things. Flak from above comes because the second-line managers know the work is done by the first-line departments and real stuff needs to happen. Besides, their next promotion depends on how well the first-line departments produce. Therefore, think carefully before you enter the ranks of management if your aspirations stop at the first rung in the hierarchy. Remember that it is difficult to break out of a first-line slot because corporations are organized like pyramids and every step is more elusive than the previous one.

A few managers get promoted into the ranks of the powerful. Impressive titles usually accompany these jobs to reinforce the importance of such positions. Once attaining such a visible position, some of these individuals forget past acquaintances whom they knew in their less omniscient worker days. It's as if they want everyone to think they never had to crawl before walking. Past peers may be treated with indifference possibly because they know the executives' prior mistakes and the executives know they know. When dealing with these managers, it may seem you need an appointment to talk about anything. But no one is that important. No one's time is that scarce. The net effect of such behavior is that former associates may feel patronized and react with apathy and disdain. A wall of non-communication and resentment may result. However, in some cases it could be easy to reverse this situation. The managers should simply treat prior associates with continued respect, and the associates will probably repay them in kind. For managers secure in their positions, this act becomes effortless.

When Management Is out of Touch with Reality

Sustained corporate profits can provide a convenient facade to hide managerial incompetence. The managers in power may delude themselves into believing that the success is because of their political cleverness, insight, and overall administrative skills. After all, the bottom line says that they are doing a good job (even though they may be, in effect, riding on the coattails of their predecessors' successes). Such happenings can go on for years even though a management has in reality become complacent, pretentious, and arrogant. Still, such managers can surround themselves with people who tell them what they want to hear to further their own personal objectives.

In this era of gamesmanship, only a drop in corporate profits can halt such a circus. When the red ink finally appears, what might a psychotic upper management do? Unfortunately, fault may be parceled out in a seemingly random fashion. Management may sloppily try to patch fundamental errors in business judgment but fail to address the real problems. For example, let's say top management thinks it can positively affect the income slide by scheduling high-level customer meetings regarding the company's future directions. Consequently, a feeling that all is good is imagined by out-of-touch managers who have come to believe that words are more important than actions. When this fails, management believes the next step is to reorganize while maintaining the existing company structure. Surely this will do the trick. It always worked in the past. No such luck. The money dive continues. The question of how best to compete with more-nimble competitors remains elusive. (Providing products and services that customers want is always a good start.) Suddenly, another brilliant idea is unleashed. A proposal to divide the company into smaller autonomous units is touted as the next panacea. After all, the competition moves fast because it is not burdened by the constraints imposed by the structure necessary to control a big organization. This approach has some merit at first glance but is outweighed by less obvious considerations. For example, if the big company was a provider of system solutions then:

↬ The resulting independent companies will now have to compete with their traditional competitors plus the ones created by the breakup. Failure can occur simply because of a misguided emphasis on doing things differently, not better.

↬ The resulting uncoordinated product line mix will most likely damage the integrated-systems image that the big company enjoyed with its customers.

So much for top management's ideas. The employees who lose most in a corporate downturn are not the big executives who receive fat salaries and lucrative buy-out contracts but rather the lower-level employees.

Remember that true management ability surfaces when things go bad. Real leaders get their hands dirty and earn the respect of their employees. They do not isolate themselves into corners of security.

How Some Managers Get Removed from Power

Occasionally managers get into trouble by not fulfilling commitments. This occurrence can result in either a discreet or an obvious ousting of the offending manager. Knowing not what to expect, most administrators under duress have discovered it is wise to give the appearance that everything is running smoothly, even when a pending disaster is on the horizon. They may think somehow things will work out, and sometimes they do. However, getting help from others (especially corporate help) is a sure way for this manager to occupy her time with endless meetings, interrogation, finger pointing, and so on. If a solution is worked out, someone else will probably take the credit, and she may be made to look incompetent. So managers in this position usually opt to just hold on.

Occasionally, a savvy high-level manager senses that all is not what it appears, so that manager uses a tested technique to really find out what's happening. Sending the suspect individual to a two-week educational course is a favorite choice. Attending a class at the corporate management school removes any interference from that manager. Eagerly, this person accepts the vacation because it offers a respite from her horrible predicament. The stage is now set to make unlimited inquiries (the formal phrase used by corporate is an *internal audit*) into the suspected department's activities. The buffering that in-trouble managers subconsciously provide is no longer present. Let's look more closely at an example of this activity.

First management usually looks at what's happening from a management perspective. The offending department's efforts may be diverted to creating charts with which to wow internal auditors. The workers usually do a good job at the chart-making because this activity is a highly developed skill in large corporations. The official audit outcome may reveal that the disaster looks repairable with a few tweaks. Now the savvy inquiring manager usually asks non-management types for their evaluation. A face-to-face discussion with the employee who is leading the shaky department's work effort may disclose that there is no way to meet commitments with the current staffing's expertise. The inquiring manager's suspicions are confirmed. Quick action is needed. Should the situation be handled discreetly, or should the offending manager be publicly purged? Experience shows that purges relay a direct message to both management types and the working employees. As for workers, they welcome situations in which managers are treated as other individuals found to be deficient in performing assigned tasks.

When the educational class is over, a review meeting may be scheduled to assess product schedules and other commitments. It may begin with an innocuous phrase like, "How are things going?" If the educational-course graduate responds with something like, "Experience has shown that if you are not ahead of schedule then you are behind schedule," this gobbledygook reply will probably immediately incur the wrath of the high-level manager, who will probably tell her in the presence of others that she has messed up big time. She may be immediately taken out of the management position and told to work third shift in a technical job about which she knows nothing. Now this is severe, but it shows everyone else that concealed disasters will be dealt with severely.

Surprisingly, such an action usually has a net positive effect on the entire area. A sense of urgency is instilled into every employee. New management is installed, and honesty creeps back into the work environment. It is a refreshing change from the game playing that seems to occupy everyone's time and effort. If the situation had been handled discreetly, like by announcing the offending manager's appointment to a "special assignment designed to broaden her background," the manager's removal would have had little impact. Employees need to see proof that incompetence has no place in the work environment.

Conclusion

The need for management will always exist whenever the efforts of groups of individuals need to be coordinated toward a common goal. So learn to live with the various structures and absurdities that go along with the administrivia world. Unfortunately, no one has come up with a good alternative. However, less is better.

Most of the management personalities you will encounter in your career will each have a dominant style characteristic and a random mixture of traits from other management types (discussed previously). Learn to cope with those you can work with, and avoid those who can inhibit your contributions and development. Just knowing the variety of styles gives you an edge in maintaining a good attitude and a healthy mental state.

Inside the Company

~ of ~

And You Thought Only People Could Get Indigestion

In general, a company's culture, structure, and business endeavors all contribute to the happenings that occur within an organization. Such things affect employees' work assignments, attitudes, and resultant contributions. However, sometimes it seems that every day gives birth to an unexpected adventure (for example, hosting a visit from the big boys from corporate), which often detracts from getting anything done. Remember that people feel comfortable knowing what to expect, and they react with some degree of displeasure whenever there is a deviation.

Other unintended irritations can occur because of a company's size, maturity, gamesmanship toleration, and inept administration of its employees. Become aware that such distractions exist and that they can all inhibit doing something real. Become acquainted with the topics discussed in the following sections so you can recognize the hazards of working for a large corporation.

Hierarchies and Large Corporations

The hierarchical structure is the accepted means to control the workings of large organizations. This applies to armies, religious groups, governments, and so on. It seems natural that companies should also be organized in this manner. In fact the hierarchy is the dominant structure in use today to control an organization of any kind. Increasingly we witness the demise of once-proud companies that are overwhelmed by newer companies unburdened by a complicated structure needed to control a large organization. In addition, the executives of newer companies tend to be leaders with high IQs. These new managers compete with their counterparts who usually have risen in large organizations by tenure, conformance, or just being good-old-boys. The latter is often void of the daring and innovation required to effectively compete.

It's no secret that most progress comes from individuals, not "managed" people in departments with fixed objectives. The bigger the company, the more management layers involved. Each of these layers must strive to prove its worth to the organization. The more management, the longer it takes to react to conditions affecting a company's products and revenue. So what do large companies do to counteract their stagnation? Why, a reorganization is often just what the doctor ordered. Managers in the old organization are placed in management slots in the new organization. Never mind that not all managers are portable. It's almost comical to experience the reorganizations that continually occur in large corporations that are hoping another management structure can succeed where the current one has failed or is expected to fail.

For companies that are somewhat static by the nature of their business, hierarchies can work for long periods of time. But for companies that need to be dynamic, hierarchies get in the way. The people on the bottom, who actually do the work, are constrained by management layers that need to justify their high-paying positions.

So what means other than hierarchical exist to control a fast-moving organization? Small companies use a *working leader,* who performs tasks just like a regular employee but also functions as a spokesperson for the group and directly or indirectly rewards individuals based on their contributions. If successful, small companies grow, but then immediately advocates of management layers usually appear. This if-you-don't-grow-you-will-die syndrome can take over a company's objectives instead of allowing the company to focus on doing the best job for its customers. A collection of loosely organized groups can get everyone nervous about being small, and eventually a growth company may give in to being "managed." The company may succeed, but eventually it will become too large, and then it will be replaced by a younger, dynamic organization. Such is the nature of large organizations. Can you name any of the non-monopolistic companies of the 1880s that exist today? It looks like there is a life cycle for companies, just as there is a life cycle for every living thing.

Rightsizing the Workplace

After the accountants have convinced management of the huge savings that will occur after employees are shed in the name of the popular euphemism *rightsizing,* the next step is to rightsize the physical plant to accommodate the remaining workers in surroundings more appropriate to their number. Office space per employee is a fertile cost-cutting field scrutinized by the company accountants. The more people per square foot, the better the bottom line on a per individual expense basis. Who can argue with such tangible facts? So the objective of these cost-conscious people is to cram as many individuals as possible into the smallest space possible.

Although these maneuvers look great on the balance sheet, intangibles such as productivity loss usually increase exponentially. For example, if the former space occupancy rate was one employee per cubicle, and now it is two or even three workers per cubicle, distractions such as increased phone conversations, interruptions by other visiting workers, discomfort caused by the heat dissipation of each individual's computer workstation, and lower morale contribute to a decrease in productivity. Also, now that there are more people per cubicle, the ratio of people to facilities such as restrooms, vending machines, and elevators may increase so dramatically that waiting lines may occur on a regular basis. So the lost time may never show up on a balance sheet. Unfortunately, the company loses without even realizing it. When will companies learn that happy workers produce more products than unhappy workers do?

Bureaucratic Signals

You don't have to wonder if you work in a bureaucratic organization— just look around. There are signals everywhere. For example, one bureaucratic signal is management overattentiveness. Nothing can kill enthusiasm and productivity more than a management that continually monitors the daily activities of people's work. Managers who excessively monitor employees have a natural tendency toward insecurity. They must be constantly reassured regarding the success of the employee's efforts. Weekly status reports, department meetings, verbal briefings, and the review of employee work by others give the manager sufficient information to place any blame directly on the employee if the project fails. Unfortunately, this keep-yourself-covered method of operation prevails in large corporations. The larger the corporation, the greater the information trail to blame someone else.

In addition, the number, size, booking rate, and elaborate furnishings of meeting rooms are all indications of a company's degree of commitment to bureaucracy. The time schedule for particular meeting rooms can even be reserved for up to a year in advance. These things all can detract from employees performing anything useful because doing real work takes a backseat to learning the meeting game. It takes time to prepare for scheduled meetings with your peers, and your perceived contributions to the company are confined to your behavior at such gatherings. Ask yourself why it is necessary to have a meeting every Tuesday at 2 p.m. to discuss topics that haven't even arisen yet. Then you will begin to realize that the meeting game is a bureaucratic end in itself.

Left alone for any period of time, people will eventually do something useful. At this time another bureaucratic attribute often invades your productive efforts: Now that you have actually done something, you need the approval of numerous individuals to continue your work. These approvals ensure the following things:

1. Your project doesn't overlap anyone else's function in the company.
2. Your project is either strategic or at least tactical. Funny thing is that down the road tactical things turn out to be strategic things.
3. Your project is put on some kind of announcement schedule to which you have little input.
4. Your project is scrutinized by professional company watchdogs. At first glance the reasons these people come up with for killing the project seem plausible. For example:
   ✧ The mass production of the automobile could have been prevented by a correct observation of a lack of roads or gas stations.
   ✧ It could have been argued that electricity in homes was not practical because of a lack of generating/transmission/distribution stations.

Unfortunately these examples of bureaucracy expand as the company matures. Corporations seem to forget that they accomplished previous successes without such things.

Products That Mirror Company Structure

Companies doing business worldwide often feel the need to locate product development sites within those countries that contribute significantly to corporate revenues. Presumably, this is done to soften the reality that a company is taking huge profits from particular countries without giving anything back. So it feels an obligation to invest some of its profits back into the local economy in the form of jobs. But if the products being manufactured at these remote locations are components of a larger product (say, a computer system), the effect can be devastating and entirely unappreciated by the people running the company. First, the language barrier may create communication problems that didn't exist when product development was centralized in only a couple of domestic locations. Remember that even if the foreign employees are practically fluent in the worldwide business language (English), humor, slang, and subtleties in tone inflection all can contribute to miscommunication. Resolving these problems has resulted in the creation of an entire class of employees who do nothing but function as facilitators. They hold meetings to attempt to resolve issues, schedule weekly teleconferences, document agreements, escalate problems of non-cooperating site locations to higher-level management, and travel to discuss product development reviews with their counterparts in other locations.

Communication that used to occur naturally and verbally among development people now involves another layer of employees (facilitators) who are looked upon as key to a product's success. The irony of this situation is that these facilitator jobs become highly coveted because they can gain their occupants visibility to upper management while removing them from the demanding task of performing real work in product development. Soon, the real workers may see that functioning as a facilitator is a much softer lifestyle than doing real work. So, some development people leave the productive ranks and become world-class wordsmith artists. Why not? It appears to be a surefire career growth path, and it looks impressive on a resume to the unknowing recruiter. But what kind of products are produced under this environment? Let's take a close look. First, development people like to isolate their components from the effect of other components so that they are not bothered by the normal changes that occur during a cycle. This is natural and good until you realize that this isolation often requires the specification of firm interfaces that become cast in concrete. Even if later there surfaces a better way to merge product components, it never happens because of the commitment to the outdated interface.

Product schedules, performance, quality, reliability, and function replication sometimes suffer because of the perception that spreading the work around will benefit the company's image. It turns out that the structure of products developed with such constraints mirrors the organization of the company that developed it. A not-so-surprising effect of such an organization is an increase in the number of employees required to function in such an environment. This leaves the company vulnerable to other corporations that are only interested in turning out the best product for the least cost. Therefore, the original product objectives often become blurred with the structure of the various product development organizations.

New Product Pitfalls

The future of high-tech companies is rooted in the reality that they must put out new products to survive in the marketplace. Planned obsolescence should be a fact of life. If you don't do it, your competition will. After all, where are the companies that built the Conestoga wagon or made buggy whips? Are new products really that innovative? Mostly the answer is no. And this is not a bad thing. But give an old product a new name prefixed with the word *turbo,* and immediately the name implies that this new product is super-fast. *Industrial strength* implies super-reliability even though the new product may be less reliable than its predecessor. In the short term, the word game may make or break a product independent of its merits. It's a high-stakes marketing word game that uses deception, euphemisms, half-truths, and outright lies to gain an advantage.

Experience teaches that good products build on the strengths of their predecessors. Evolutionary changes should be welcomed by the marketplace. Instead, the most publicity is usually reserved for companies making the most outlandish claims for their all-new super whiz-bang products. Why should something new always be thought of as better than something old? Probably it's part of our culture, which favors youth over maturity. In reality, something brand new is usually accompanied with many problems. Customers stuck buying such products are often told that, because the products are on the leading edge of technology, they should expect to encounter such anomalies. The negatives are sometimes further softened with phrases like, "Executives at the highest levels are aware of your problem," "This problem has been assigned the highest priority," or even "We are sparing no expense to bring this problem to a conclusion" when what is needed is someone at the worker level who knows how to fix the problems. What usually happens is that executives at the producing and consuming end discuss the failings of new products in abstract terms without really understanding what they are talking about. When a problem is eventually assigned to someone who can fix it, these same executives may feel a high degree of accomplishment because their egos tell them they helped solve the problem.

Does the best product always excel over the competition? Actually no. The winner is usually the product that is first to the market with the solution or the product that became the established standard because of sheer numbers. Take Sony's Beta Max videocassette recorder (VCR), a perfect example of a product that had technical superiority over the VHS technology, which eventually prevailed as the industry standard in the battle for VCR tape format. What does prevail is whoever does the best job of selling. Companies have learned this lesson well. You don't have to market the best technical product to succeed.

The Art of the Schedule

In some large corporations, the importance of product schedules assumes the rigidity of a concrete structure. Conversely, some schedules change based on the latest power play made by a high-level manager in a meeting with marketing people who wanted everything yesterday. The concrete version of a time commitment may even be placed in an employee's personnel jacket to be reviewed at her next performance evaluation. Meeting a schedule may even take precedence over the content and quality of a person's assignment because such promises are an easy way to measure a person's job contribution, whereas product function and quality usually cannot be adequately evaluated until after customers experience its use. An employee's association with an inferior product is easy to forget after it is shipped. Unfortunately, those responsible for a product's development phase are usually not involved in responding to customer complaints regarding its deficiencies. They are long gone, working on the next development product. Enter the words *retrofit* and *improved version*. These terms are frequently used to soothe a complaining customer with a promise to bring the deficient product up to expectations. Unfortunately, management has begun to rely on the fact that new versions and retrofits are a normal part of the cycle. This makes the scheduling part of a job even more important.

In some instances schedules are created without the participation of the employee who will be responsible for fulfilling such a commitment. A manager operating in this mode usually assumes that he knows more than the employee does in this regard. Most veteran workers, however, take pledges measured in time seriously because they know management takes this aspect of job performance seriously. Inexperienced employees often seem to have the attitude, "It'll be done when it's done." However, it only takes one missed commitment to become a seasoned worker. Missed schedules follow you around like an anathema—especially when it comes time to list your accomplishments in a quest for a raise or promotion. Some tactics managers often use to secure schedule commitments are as follows:

- ☞ They may inform you that your peers have already committed to the schedule.
- ☞ They may inform you that company profits are based on fulfilling a commitment within a certain time frame.
- ☞ They may emphasize to you that other parts of the product depend on your tight time commitment.

Employees can even be caught off guard by managers' simple ploy of presenting the schedule commitment as preliminary. Your manager may say, "It's a stake in the ground" (a beginning point) or "It can be changed later when you know more about what you are committing to." However, later you may discover that once a "preliminary" commitment becomes known, your manager, your manager's manager, and so on assume the commitment is unchangeable.

Schedules contain periodic checkpoints, meant to monitor the progress of people's efforts toward fulfilling a time commitment. Elaborate charts are often constructed to show a schedule's intricate details. At times it appears as if product schedule charts are more important than the actual work being performed. As people soon learn, chartsmanship has become an extremely important asset for an employee in any large corporation.

Schedule Slippage

If a person cannot possibly meet a schedule, a favorite tactic is to look for another employee, manager, or circumstance to "take the fall" for any schedule delay. Events that may be entirely unrelated to whether a person completes a schedule can be "saved" as a defense tactic when it becomes obvious that she cannot meet the committed date. E-mail, memos, meeting notes, and documented conversations can be used for this purpose. In large corporations, this gathering of slippage data seems a natural part of the job, just in case. Some astute maneuvering often occurs whenever a slippage in schedule happens, for example:

- ☞ Fostering the illusion that you have met your committed date by delivering (to a verification department) an incomplete version of a product to gain a couple of more days of time. You know that the receiving department will need time to unravel the supplied materials before it can truly evaluate what you sent. In the case of a software product commitment, you can use the excuse that there must have been a transmission error when the product was copied to some storage media, like a tape. No one really knows the truth for sure, and you have gained time without admitting to a missed commitment. Of course, as soon as you become aware of the discrepancy, you should state that you will send a fresh copy immediately.

↦ Delivering the product to a sister department a couple of days late and deliberately placing it in an obscure location. Then you can make an inquiry about the department's experience using the product. When it responds that it has not yet received the product, you can state that you delivered it last week and that it can be found in a corner at the end of the hallway. You can give the appearance that you are upset about the delay. You can then suggest that perhaps the sister department would like an updated version because the integration process has not yet begun.

Sometimes the stakes are high, especially when multiple companies are working on the same project. Company A says all of its commitments are on schedule, hoping that Company B finally admits that it cannot meet its commitments. This will be confirmed when Company B's completion date passes without anything being delivered. Everyone may be in time trouble, but no one will dare admit it. All are hoping that another will be found out before they are. Such is the schedule slippage phenomenon.

Success Breeds Complacency

Companies that have enjoyed success for long periods of time tend to believe this occurs because of management's astute handling of the business. However, in a number of instances Company X actually enjoys some niche advantage or may even border on a type of monopoly. Still, it seems the company succeeds no matter what it does. The executives of such a company often begin to believe they are invincible and develop an extreme sense of hubris. They are quoted in the trade journals, are featured in financial magazines, and may even serve on government committees. They become the model executives of corporate life. The longer this euphoria continues, the more out of touch with reality the company's future becomes. Work that has been outsourced to smaller companies (because of some accountant's urging) soon gives rise to the common worker's realization that the contracted company is the one that understands the needs of the customer, not the bureaucrats who think they are managing yet another successful project. This scenario has occurred many times during the last century, but companies still refuse to recognize it while it is happening. Signs of complacency include the following:

- Emphasizing office trappings (wood furniture, windows with a view, and so on)
- Assigning fancy job titles (like worldwide planning executive for intergalactic communication) with nebulous responsibility
- Frequently traveling to distant company locations that have nothing to do with the job at hand
- Pretending to be busy when there is little to do
- Implementing dress codes that emphasize neatness
- Separating a manager's office from the department's workers (perhaps by putting the manager on an aisle containing only executive offices)
- Defining lines of responsibility so that decisions require multiple levels of concurrence (often responsibilities are distributed to locations in different states and then to different countries)
- Emphasizing that international currency fluctuations are the reason for sub-par performance during a downturn in company profits
- Maintaining large staffs of people who pander to corporate executives' whims
- Repeating certain brief terms and phrases in any situation to sound important, for example:
  1. Staffing plan alternatives
  2. Impact assessment
  3. Understand the needs of the customer
  4. Back to basics
  5. Readjust priorities
  6. Resource alignment
  7. Check my calendar
  8. Brief me
  9. Schedule alternatives

Soon it becomes evident to the contracting company that it can offer a competing product that the marketplace wants instead of a product that has been edicted by the big corporation. When threatened by the smaller company, the large corporation may even deride the quality of the competition's products. Then the large corporation may say the niche market of the competitor's products is not worth the attention of the big corporation. Finally, the large corporation may slowly realize that, yes indeed, the smaller company does present formidable competition. By then it's too late because the marketplace has already chosen its champion for the foreseeable future—the smaller company.

The Effect of Success on Management and the Company

Frequently, the success of a company in the marketplace shrouds a person in the corporation (or many people—especially the management) with the illusion that he is one terrific employee. This feeling can last for years. However, close scrutiny often reveals that this person or these persons probably had nothing to do with the company's good fortune. Still they may assume an air of superiority that makes others think they are successful, skillful individuals. In reality, companies that border on being monopolies or possess some other business anomaly that gives them a marketplace advantage are nothing new. The trick is for employees to objectively evaluate their real contributions.

But history is seldom visited by the successful (usually only failures look at the past to learn from their mistakes). This air of superiority can flow into their private lives with such perks as new cars and fancy vacations. They may live beyond their abilities. They want and need others to perceive them as having "made it." Usually, the longer the success of a company endures, the further management's perception of its abilities wanders from reality. They only have to test the job market to find out their real worth. But this rarely happens when people are on the success bandwagon. The company often will interpret low employee turnover as an indication of the superiority of its personnel department rather than realizing that employees know a good thing when they see it. And success causes inbreeding because, after all, why look for new employees outside the company when its past successes say that the best people are already employed?

After the passage of time, the company is overflowing with senior people (age and position) still basking in past glories. The bright new college graduates have been hired by the competition for so long that the company's recruiters may be shunned on campuses around the country. The day of reckoning arrives when the company's balance sheet begins to show signs of red ink. The company's top management may start blaming fluctuations in international currency rates, the sluggish European economy, the general business downturn, or whatever—just so it doesn't appear as if anything management has control over is at fault. Still reality has not caught on. Perhaps the company needs some new marketing buzzwords to beef up revenue. Catchy phrases like *world class, conformance to international standards, corporate restructuring, market driven,* and so on are touted as the answer to the company's problems. Slowly reality sinks in. The company recognizes that the real problem is management itself. Then, almost overnight, a determined search is initiated to hire someone who can turn the business around. Panic drives the business. Long-term direction gives way to matching the competition. A me-too attitude pervades the company. Product leadership is forgotten, and so are the things that made the company successful in the first place. Funny thing—previously the company stated that its people were its most important resource. Now the attitude is to shed as many people as possible through methods such as rightsizing.

The Centralized Management Folly

Large corporations often feel the need to control decentralized company-development sites with corporate staffs whose sole purpose is to keep up with what's going on at the producing locations. This can have devastating effects on the speed, expense, and efficiency of product development. Because the corporate staff isn't responsible for producing anything, its primary activity is to hold meetings, talk on the telephone, congregate around the coffee machines, and so on—if just to take up enough time to constitute a day's work. This type of organization has a hidden effect on the producing employees because they see that the high-paying, high-exposure positions are not related to doing anything real but merely track what producers do. If the corporation enjoys a near monopoly in the marketplace, then this activity can continue for decades because no outside competition will challenge the inefficiencies of how large corporations function.

Sadly, the best career-growth path in this instance is for a producing employee to quit doing real work and keep the corporate staffers informed about what's going on, while hoping she will be recognized as a valuable employee who should be promoted to a corporate position. Of course what happens is that a producer now becomes a permanent non-producer. Ironic but sadly true. Once attaining such a position, individuals may suddenly begin quoting executives with such phrases as, "John thinks we should improve the delivery schedule." Of course "we" implies those responsible for doing something and at the same time raises the perception others have of the aspiring staffee, as it appears she is on a first-name basis with John, the division president.

Workers make individual decisions regarding their willingness to play this corporate game. Those who recognize the game playing for what it is can get some degree of satisfaction in doing relevant work, but in doing so their careers can become limited. Those who choose the corporate ladder often must live with the insecurities of possessing no marketable skills outside the corporation and the knowledge that they may be despised by long-term doers.

Centralized management also likes to promote the perception that only it can initiate new products, can analyze the marketplace, and in general has the necessary wherewithal to do any strategic planning. This type of thinking can stifle people at the worker level who know what's going on. Developers know both the positive and the negative aspects of their products and also how the products stack up against those of the competition. In large companies these people are seldom given the opportunity to influence the direction of their products, about which no one knows more. Even if centralized management is correct in its thinking, it takes years for its influence to affect what goes on at the worker level. Consequently, real workers may abandon the corporate game and seek smaller companies where they can have an impact.

Non-obvious Multi-location Anomalies

Many corporations pondering the location of new development and manufacturing facilities prefer places off the beaten path. These locations provide many benefits not apparent to the casual observer. In particular, northern climates offer advantages to a company that has manufacturing and development sites in various parts of the country. In the winter months, darkness may still be present during the employees' drive to work. Upon entering the workplace, the employee gets a positive boost in attitude for the day ahead from the illuminated environment because light provides a kind of visual stimulation that darkness hides. An added pleasure is that the workplace temperature is maintained at a comfort level that satisfies a person's physical need of warmth. The work environment thus provides a feeling of security when the employee looks out the window at the cold winter day. It becomes a refuge from Mother Nature's harsh elements. Even working overtime is not that unpleasant because it provides an excuse for postponing the entry into darkness once again.

Recruiting for an out-of-the-way northern company site presents some challenges that are not present in recruiting for warm-weather locations. Airline transportation, cultural activities, shopping, and so on may all be deficient. The company's strategy to combat this list of negatives is to emphasize the advantages of a small community. Low crime, good schools, and family-oriented company activities help sway job candidates to choose a life that most likely offers stability and a better-than-average opportunity. Now, let's look at the negatives, which are not so apparent to the new college hire. Social activities for young singles can be severely limited in these small northern communities. The need of the new college hire to meet other individuals in the same marital state can be so strong that it can easily stimulate a request for a transfer to another company location. Quite expectedly such a request will be ignored, delayed, and obstructed as much as possible because the company needs to discourage this course of action; it could turn into a deluge. Finding another job in another company offers the best solution for people in this situation. Presumably such individuals are young, have not established firm roots, and can take a chance on the next job working out.

Other reasons to seek employment outside the company also exist, but in a small-town company-dominated atmosphere, you need to consider other variables. The opportunities to get another position that can utilize your acquired skills in the same small town is most likely severely limited. A new job then means a physical move to another city. It's not like taking a different route to work on Monday morning. Rather, your whole life will change. It's a tough decision—new schools for the children, new neighbors, new shopping, new medical providers, new everything. Such change causes stress. These considerations work in the company's favor because they actually contribute to a low employee turnover rate. Now consider what will happen if the company decides to reduce its work force. Fired or laid-off employees are in an even worse position because immediate action is required on their part. At this time individuals are painfully reminded that their network of job acquaintances consists of people who work for the same company. The company has a kind of captive work force.

The fact that the company is the only game in town contributes to the loyalty that people feel toward their employer. However, never let loyalty take a backseat to objectivity. Games change, attitudes change, and companies change.

Some Pitfalls of Bigness

The very nature of bigness leads to the eventual deterioration of companies that once led their fields of endeavor. The size of a corporation greatly influences its organizational structure This in turn affects the number of management layers, the number of physical locations, the variety of products produced, the duplication of function because of replicated sites, and even the countries in which these sites reside. You see, politics often sways site location because business acumen dictates that the prosperity of the company should be shared with nations that contribute large profits to the companies coffers. Eventually the speed with which a company can develop new products may shift into low gear because of the number of processes the corporation has in place to manage its complex enterprise. Smaller competitors, unburdened with bigness, are often better able to react to market conditions with delivered goods and services that may even have been invented by the slow moving giant. How ironic!

One of the most exaggerated tools management has pounced upon to manage its bigness is a *process.* This mechanism is useful to some extent. However, the degree to which today's companies adhere to this device overwhelms common sense. For example, companies often reason that if the process works for a manufacturing operation, then why not apply it to the ranks of professional workers? A surge in the frequency of department meetings discussing the processes its members should follow is meant to impregnate employees to this way of thinking. These processes are blessed by management—do or die—everyone must follow them. An international standards committee may even exist to check to see if a company is following the defined processes. Awards may be given for adhering to these principles. Most employees scoff at all this hoopla deep inside while externalizing an appearance of compliance. Immediate management may sense that all is not well with this new tool but usually does nothing to rock the boat. Being a member of the team takes precedence over facing reality.

For jobs that require judgment, it would be far better for companies to state expectations in clear terms such as quality level, schedule, performance, and cost. Then they should let employees help define the processes that work best for them to achieve the end result. Whatever works for one employee may not work for another. Management of professionals needs to realize that employees are people, each with a personality of his or her own. This is where the commodity treatment of workers by Human Resources (one of Webster's definitions for a resource is "available money or property") and an obedient management staff contribute to the chaos and deterioration of once leading-edge corporations.

Bigness begets rules and corporations rely on these precepts (written or verbal, implied or explicit) to make their jobs easier. Better to refer to a rule book than make a decision on one's own initiative. Have you tired of hearing, "company policy says . . ."? It's a favorite crutch used in large companies. Remember, however, that rules have a way of changing, especially when they affect profits.

To simply manage the activities of a large enterprise, corporations have found it necessary to maintain rule books and conform to defined standards *(processes)* by which the companies' products and services are produced and provided. In their quest for uniformity and control, this accepted practice has led to mind-inhibiting mechanisms that turn off any initiative for doing a job faster and/or more efficiently. Is it any wonder that smaller companies always seem to overtake a slow-moving giant?

Decision Making

When it becomes necessary to make a decision, the individual who makes the decision becomes identified with that choice only if he and others believe that such a decision is clearly correct. However, management can use numerous ploys to disassociate itself from a wrong decision. These techniques are as follows:

- *Shared decision making* can distribute any wrongdoing among other people who may or may not have had a role in arriving at the decision. Meetings are a tool employed to distribute responsibility (hence the phrase, "The consensus of the meeting was . . ."). Unfortunately, the individuals who participated in such a meeting often are never identified. Actually, shared decision making is a method preferred by managers to avoid the stigma of being a loner or a wild duck. After all, management involves team players and a happy community of the good-old-boy life. If by chance a correct decision is made during a meeting, then a phenomenon known as the eye doctor syndrome (I evaluated, I coordinated, I proposed, I understood,) may occur if a seasoned meeting individual claims responsibility for any positive result that occurred.
- Claiming that *incorrect input* contributed to the wrong decision shifts the blame to individuals who were consulted for their opinions and expertise. In this manner it appears that the manager was duped, and she can retaliate by publicizing the imprecise, misleading, or missing data that led to her decision. Corporate people tend to forget that management's role is to take all input (good, bad, and missing) and to evaluate it so an informed decision can be made. If there is not sufficient information to make a decision, then the manager should ask for more data. Pressure to make a decision when there is not

adequate data is a specious managerial complaint. After all, managers are paid to take risks and for their insight into such matters when they do not have all the facts.

↬ The *conditions-have-changed syndrome* is a technique especially favored by individuals working in marketing or requirements positions who have neglected a particular duty assigned to them. Because they didn't do their jobs in the first place, they now have an opportunity to redirect work that has been in progress for some time. Consider this scenario: A company's workers are dedicated to developing a new product when they suddenly learn that it is not the product customers want. (Unfortunately, it is difficult to argue with such a position because it involves a prediction of external factors that require interpretation by the company's soothsayers. It's hard to argue against a prediction of the future, even if your gut feel tells you otherwise.) In this situation, the individual who promotes the conditions-have-changed syndrome appears to be on top of things. It seems that only by his astute investigations did this new information surface at all. This new news is greeted with enthusiasm, especially by people who were behind in their production schedules. Everyone breathes a sigh of relief, and work begins anew on the new set of market requirements.

↬ *Decision by default* occurs when management is afraid to make a decision or doesn't even understand that a decision is needed. Then if the default decision fails, management can claim it is not to blame. Decisions by default occur especially in companies where changes occur rapidly because managers have a tendency to become isolated from the advancing real world. Workers whose job it is to produce something will do just that, independent of any direction from above.

↬ *Decision by technical anointment* occurs when a company-backed technical guru insists that only she understands what is needed in the marketplace. Technical gurus usually have a low degree of tolerance for anyone who disagrees with their direction, even though most real workers disagree with it when the gurus are not present. To disagree with a company-anointed guru would jeopardize one's career, and everyone knows it. Only individuals who are on the same or a higher level within the company may openly disagree with a guru decision. However, this almost never happens because of the tacit don't-tell-on-me-and-I-won't-tell-on-you syndrome.

Human Resources and Perceptions

Not surprisingly, physical attributes play a large part in the selection of Human Resources (HR) Department staff members. External appearances (height, weight, grooming, dress, mannerisms) are the first thing people experience when they come in contact with a member of HR. Verbal externals in an HR employee are also important because these attributes communicate many things. For example, a deep-sounding male voice indicates decisiveness, power, energy, and other traits associated with success. The ability to express one's viewpoints in an eloquent manner verifies experience, depth, and other positive thoughts. Therefore, this people-oriented function is stocked with men and women who possess superior visuals and audibles.

Because job applicants' memories of meeting a company's HR reps influence the applicants' desire to work for the company, corporations understand that they have a self-serving interest in doing all that is necessary to have HR people reflect favorably on their enterprises. Even if an organization does not hire a particular applicant, it is important that he retains an approving image of the company. He will most certainly relate his initial experience to others (especially classmates on the college campus). Therefore, companies view anything that can assist in this perception as a positive.

Your initial impression of the HR encounter carries over into the first years of your employment with that company. The company wants you to perceive that the HR function is independent from the internal company machinations and that it is there to safeguard your interests. You may be led to believe that the HR Department monitors management practices to see that employees are treated fairly. You may be led to believe that HR tracks peer industry salaries to ensure that your compensation (salary, benefits) remains equal to or above that offered by the competition. In effect you probably will be constantly bombarded with propaganda that tells you how good life is working for Company X. In practice, however, you may begin to discover contradictions, inconsistencies, and deception. For example, the hundred-hour weeks that you are working to complete a time-critical project may have come to the attention of HR, but not out of HR's concern for your physical and mental health. Rather, the company may be violating some state or federal labor regulation. In addition you may be making an excessive amount of money. Any disturbance to the corporation's income differential between the manager class and non-manager class becomes an irritation that HR views with disdain.

Later in corporate life (after you have passed age forty and presumably are less job-marketable), you may feel you are being taken advantage of. You may complain to management that family and other non-company-related involvements suffer from your long absences caused by work commitments made by others. You will probably be told in the most eloquent language (authored by someone skilled in the use of human resource terminology), "This is a business," "You make good money," and "If you don't like it, then quit." Deep inside you probably know that your immediate management is not capable of such articulation. Besides, this frequent complaint begs for a well-rehearsed response. You may suspect Human Resources has been consulted. You are probably right. HR (with assistance from the company legal wizards) is adept at concocting a series of euphemisms that get a point across without violating government employment regulations.

Human Resources and Corporate Hiring

Staffing professional employment vacancies in large corporations is one of the main services provided by the Human Resources Department. However, rarely will a person whose availability is brought to the attention of HR by a current employee be hired. Most hiring occurs as a result of regularly scheduled recruiting trips to the nation's college campuses. The actual interview with an HR representative often reveals little to the interviewee about the available openings other than vague requirements. The HR rep usually tries to make the job description sound like a smooth transition from college to corporate life. At this point the applicant must realize that HR is functioning as a front man for management, which possesses the open hiring slots. The interviewer's knowledge is most likely sparse, so the conversation must remain at a comfort level tacitly agreed to by both HR and the applicant. External attributes are important in this phase of the interview process. Therefore, an applicant must present an impressive appearance. If HR doesn't recommend a particular candidate for a follow-up visit, the game is basically over.

Companies say they like to hire recent graduates because they are more flexible in their expectations of the work environment. Companies also popularize the seemingly innocent notion that young people's work habits closely match the requirements of the company. The translation of this statement is that, as a college student, you worked long hours for free. As a corporate employee, you are now being paid real money, and the overtime hours (at first compensated) seem like the college homework experience. You believe this corporate culture stuff is not all that bad. The company hopes this tempo will take hold and last for the duration of your career.

To lend a semblance of preciseness and objectivity to the hazy art of recruiting, HR may even rely on a series of tests that are supposed to predict a candidate's success or failure. But remember that no test can measure abstract characteristics like desire or creativity.

HR's Contribution to Confusion

Occasionally a large corporation needs experienced individuals to fill immediate needs. The local HR function comes to the rescue by placing ads in newspapers in locations known to have skilled workers employed by various companies. Because the corporation has grown so large, a strange anomaly has been known to occur: The newspaper ad appears in a city where the local company branch is experiencing an excess of employees. Without the benefit of HR coordination, one location is pushing people out the door, while another location of the same parent company has employment openings. Companies may even defend this happening by saying there were no skill matches in that city. Don't believe it. Even HR groups are not immune to the maladies associated with bigness.

Bigness: A Breeding Ground for Specialization

The lure of working for a big company stems from name recognition, stability, a defined career path, status, cost-of-living raises, imagined job security, and other such attributes. Initially, employees' job assignments are challenging because they offer new experiences. It's like an adventure into the unknown. Soon the tasks become routine, and individuals become comfortable in their new environment. Family, financial responsibilities, and lifestyle all contribute to making people content with their place in the corporate world.

Because of the size of a large company, the duties of employees become *naturally* restricted by the organizational structure necessary to manage large groups of people. Tasks are split finely to ensure that mistakes are unlikely. Too much is at stake. The resulting jobs include checkers for checkers, doers, and do-overers ad nauseam. This often makes managers protective of their areas of responsibility, and so they may limit their work scopes to ensure that what they do is done as best they can. They usually believe it is better to make no mistakes with some minor successes than to make one or two mistakes with many successes. Unfortunately, people always seem to remember the negatives.

A person's infringement into functional areas outside his assigned tasks is often looked upon with contempt and as an utter disregard for the rules of the game. Therefore, the structure to manage bigness and the resultant attitudes provide a perfect breeding ground for work specialization. Why is specialization bad? To begin with, specialized workers are not critical to the company. They are easily replaced by other specialists because the nature of the job is bounded and most likely documented as some cog in the corporate process. Many talented individuals become stuck in narrow jobs that offer absolutely no challenge. They stay because of imagined security popularized by a company that tells employees what they want to hear. Next, specialization is bad because employees limit their opportunities both within and outside the company. Small companies especially want people who can do many things. It's not a case of "My end of the boat isn't sinking." It's more like a case of "Do what it takes to get the job done." Is it any wonder that innovation and smallness are close relatives?

Ironically, large corporations have come to realize that generalists are more valuable than multitudes of specialists. Why is this true? A rounded employee can provide viewpoints that are directly attributable to her variety of experience. A rounded career in sales, manufacturing, engineering, or whatever is certainly more valuable than one spent meeting a sales quota. To this end, some progressive corporations attempt to provide this round-out to employees in the form of temporary fast-track assignments in various areas that are supposed to provide experience, perspective, and maturity. Often, what actually happens is that such anointed individuals end up not really being responsible for anything because everyone knows they will be gone in a short time to take advantage of their well-roundedness in another position. In spite of this, they usually receive favorable recommendations because the managerial staff knows they are destined for stardom and may become their boss a couple of years down the road.

The Corporate Arabesque: A Breeding Ground for the Unexpected

The fact that corporations employ huge numbers of people directly contributes to the procedures within which such organizations operate. Above all, it is necessary to project an image of fairness and equality. Anything less might cause more-stringent government scrutiny. Unfortunately, some lesser-known company practices can demoralize talented employees and even members of their families. Let's take a closer look at some finesses that occur.

The Rule Change Tactic

Let's say the company advertises that it offers a chance for winning a college scholarship. The contest is open to any child of an employee, and the winners are to be determined by SAT scores, grade point averages, class standing, activities, and the like. So far there is no cause for concern. What could be better than a competitive selection process? The final choice is made by an outside, unbiased, professional company specializing in such matters. Then let's say you are told that your child is one of the winners. "Great," you say. Here's where the company arabesque may surface. The competitive selection process may now be superseded by another set of rules. You may learn that the amount of the award is based on the income of the parent. The more you earn, the less money your child receives for the scholarship. In effect, your child can be severely penalized for having you as a parent. The amount of the award is now based on need, not scholastic excellence.

The actual financial damage can be quite severe. Let's say the compensated dollar amount ranges from 25 percent to 100 percent of a specified maximum amount. Unexpectedly, the company may determine that your child qualifies for the minimum (25 percent) scholarship. It's irritating that children of highly paid executives will get the same amount. You are not even a manager, and the company places you in the highest salary group. The details of the determination may never be revealed.

Some Promotion Gimmicks

The company makes a big play when it states that all promotions and raises are based on merit. It's kind of like school where the best students receive the highest grades. Looks good so far. Nothing could be fairer than being in competition with your peers. However, after some period has elapsed, you may discover that promotions and raises are *managed* just like everything else in a big company. To earn a promotion, you commonly must spend a required amount of time in your current job classification. Having satisfied this criterion, you then might learn that too many employees currently occupy the level to which you want to advance. Unfortunately, you may have earned a promotion, but you must wait until a slot opens up. OK, you are beginning to appreciate the way the promotion game is played. Next you may learn there is an additional roadblock. Some managed promotions require the approval of other managers in peer departments. It's the company's version of the back-scratching game: "I'll let you promote Joe Employee if you approve the promotion of one of my subordinates." This process assures that employees tend to move along at the same pace.

Most large companies think there should be no stars in their corporations. This would detract from the corporate image of a no-name work force. The company wants to keep the names of outstanding contributors confidential to ward off any outside job offers. The company also delights in the perception that no one is irreplaceable. It's the corporation, not its employees, that is important. To combat the ill feeling created by this no-stars practice, management often insists that recognition without regard to seniority is built into the merit system of promotion. To assist in this illusion, the company may permit a few token employees to be promoted earlier than normal.

A Benefit-Reduction Tactic

Sometimes a company can use its equality policy to its advantage. It can even cause a decrease in its benefit expenses. For example, let's say a husband and wife are both employed by the same enterprise. A double reimbursement for the same sickness is obviously an exploitation of the benefit. There is merit in placing a cap at 100 percent coverage. It does not seem ethical to make money by being sick. However, a corporation's medical costs can be reduced simply because two of its workers happen to be married to each other. The company accomplishes this by calculating the medical benefits as if only one individual were employed. It's kind of like only being able to collect on a single insurance policy when an insured person dies. Sound unbelievable? Remember, what the company giveth, the company can take away.

The Commitment Ploy

Management constantly pressures its employees for commitments. These can be in the form of a schedule, a function, quality, or whatever. The important thing to realize is that once a promise is made, you are on the hook. Saying you will do your best is not enough. Your reputation, compensation, and sometimes career are at stake whether you realize it or not. Other employees, departments, and managers make their commitments based on your pledge. You may even think you are covering all bases when you hedge a commitment with a series of assumptions. You may believe that if any of your suppositions are not met, then all bets are off. Think again. Such conjectures can be quickly forgotten. When promises are pitched to others, there is usually no accompanying dependency list. You may be told you are lucky you were given the opportunity even to be consulted on such matters. Sometimes others make commitments for you without your knowledge. When pressed for a commitment, think of all the things that can go wrong:

- ✎ Your manager could get another job.
- ✎ One or more of your dependencies may not be met.
- ✎ You could get sick for a week or two.
- ✎ You may be asked to make what you think is a simple extension to a committed function.
- ✎ You may be given more people to improve your schedule. (Beware of this maneuver. Remember the frequently quoted phrase of humorists, "If it takes nine months to have a baby, putting nine women to work on it can produce a child in one month.")
- ✎ You may be temporarily loaned out to another department to help in a crisis.

Commitments are necessary; just be aware of their misuse.

Failed Communication

Companies consider excellent communication the main tool to build trust between management and its many employees. They know it's important. They know employees believe it builds teamwork. What many companies fail to realize is that *how, when* and *where* information is conveyed is just as important as *what* information is declared. (However, companies sometimes err on all counts simultaneously.) If communication is not done in good taste, it usually backfires and can achieve a totally unexpected result. A classic example of failed communication is the Big Brother backlash. This maneuver starts with management's desire to push the envelope of employee communication to its limits. In this situation the company believes real-time information is better than company/industry news posted on bulletin boards, filtered through department meetings, or cleverly leaked to downplay the effect of something unpleasant. Strategically placed TV monitors in the cafeteria and outside elevator entrances appear to be excellent communication vehicles because they look high tech and appear to not take any time away from the normal work day.

In the Big Brother implementation, workers are greeted with TV screens blasting the company news, just when they thought they were about to enjoy time away from the daily grind. At lunchtime, employees get their first news glimpse while waiting for the elevator. In the cafeteria the TV screens unmercifully continue the bombardment. The TVs seem to be everywhere. Employees rightfully resent this intrusion into their private time. After all, mealtime is usually unpaid!

This transgression against the *how, when* and *where* of communication is then followed by the *what* infraction. The activities of the corporation's competitors dominate the broadcast. It appears as if the majority of accomplishments are done elsewhere. Perhaps management thought a dose of reality would motivate its employees. No such luck. After all, employees work on products and services that are directed by the management. If anything, this constant reminder of the competition's success increases the criticism toward the people calling the shots. The effect on employees is to depress their spirit and rob them of any motivation. On the way back to the office, individuals get a final blast when they step out of the elevator. Morale sinks lower. People dread the coming afternoon.

Day after day this stuff continues, but the company thinks it is doing a great job of communicating. Finally, such antics come to an abrupt end. The workers have successfully communicated to company officials that their new information distribution methods were not working. Big Brother is shut down. As usual, when a management snafu occurs, there is no mention of *why* it was necessary to change tactics. Perhaps if no one says anything, it will appear as if nothing were amiss.

Other examples of failed communication include the following:

➭ Massaged half-truths
➭ Knowledge that surfaces in the public domain before the company reveals it to its employees
➭ Information that is imprecise and intended to blur reality (this leads to various interpretations and confusion)

Conclusion

The internal machinations of successful corporations are usually overlooked so long as prosperity continues. Only financial disappointment can expose some of the nonsense that happens within the facade of a smooth-running organization. Then no sacred cows escape the scrutiny of a hatchet-wielding savior.

The Mistreatment
of Employees

~ or ~

What the Company Giveth,
the Company Can Taketh Away

Responsibilities of individuals employed in the Human Resources Department include hiring, firing, approving promotions, and arbitrating disputes between management and workers. The prior term for this function was the Personnel Department. However, many companies have deliberately chosen to change this name to a more impersonal one—Human Resources Department. This name change gives workers the message that they are considered an unfeeling resource, just like furniture, buildings, and typewriters, enforcing the notion that management considers employees just one of the many cogs in its business. The term *commodity* is most appropriate.

A prospective applicant's first encounter with a person representing a particular company is usually with an individual from the Human Resources Department. Testing, background checks, class ranking, job qualifications, and so on are all considered by HR when interviewing potential new hires. Now HR staff members do not want to make a mistake, so they follow the safe hiring path. By this I mean:

⤳ They only recommend people with a certain grade point average, say above a 3.5 average. It's the safe play.
⤳ They only recommend people who score a minimum on the company's tests (analytical, psychological, and so on), say above the 90th percentile.
⤳ They only recommend people who appear to be all-American types.
⤳ They only recommend people from schools, geographical locations, and backgrounds that have provided successful employees in the past.

Now who can blame HR if new hires fail in their job performance? Really, no one tries to argue the point, so Human Resources is safe. The trouble is that only the conventional person has a chance at being hired, when most progress depends on the unconventional individual.

Human Resources also becomes involved when an individual is subject to firing. After all, HR wants to see that the employee is treated fairly. Really? The perception that is fostered is that the employee is responsible for his termination because management certainly did everything in its power to rehabilitate this wayward individual. Never mind that the employee's manager might have been incompetent, abrasive, immoral, or unjust. The lesson here is that Human Resources staff members serve the management in power because it effectively pays their salaries. When the employee finally leaves the company, he is asked several questions, all aimed at protecting the company from any adverse effect. This is obvious from statements such as, "Do you want to retire?" (he may have been forced out and has no other alternative) and "Sign this legally binding statement to receive your severance pay" (by doing so he relinquishes his right to sue the company). So beware of the dehumanizing function called Human Resources.

The Universally Skilled Employee

Management in most large corporations holds some misconceptions regarding work, people, and skill level. One misconception in particular is that if a job description calls for a person at a particular pay grade level, say within the engineering division, then that person can perform equally well at a diversity of jobs at the same level without any training or education. How ridiculous this appears to intelligent workers. This assumption only further erodes respect for leadership. This attitude is especially prevalent in situations such as the following:

> ✤ Taking a manager from one business area (say a marketing manager) and making her responsible for staffing a programming area, which she will manage.
> ✤ Transferring a long-time manager to a technical job level even though the manager hasn't done anything technical for years.

The Specious Policy of Escalated Grievances

In the professional employee environment, when an employee believes he has been mistreated, he expresses his grievances to management. If the grievance cannot be resolved by his immediate superiors, then what to do? Of course modern management has foreseen this event and has popularized notions like grievance escalation. This is a policy whereby an employee can discuss his problem with anyone in the management chain, even the company president. Grievance escalation is intended to make the regular employees believe in the benevolence of their organization and to foster the notion of a happy family. After all, happy people produce more work than unhappy people. Such a procedure is designed to disarm an employee's hostility, and experience shows that it works. Companies emphasize that no one will be aware of an employee's grievance except the management involved, and above all, the employee's career will not be adversely affected in any way. On the surface this looks like a great plan. In reality the employee becomes a marked individual. After all, what manager wants an employee whose actions may cast a dark cloud over his own abilities to handle personal problems at the department level? The employee is treated as a leper, no matter if his issue was valid or not. Other employees are made to believe that that particular employee seriously breached the manager-employee relationship. Eventually, the employee may even quit, leaving the desired impression on other workers that it doesn't pay to make waves.

As the company matures, this escalated one-on-one procedure is usually modified in the name of freeing higher-level management's time. In reality it relieves management of any responsibility in matters of conflict, and soon the policy of the touted one-on-one procedure is handled by a committee. As an employee, you then present your grievances to a nebulous group of people wishing to gain favor with upper management by dealing harshly with such matters. Remember that in matters of disagreement with company management, the full company resources (legal, Human Resources, upper management, and so on) are at the disposal of your adversary. In contrast, you—as a man on an island—are left to your own fate. Experience shows that only a fool represents himself in any legal dispute. This is why the great majority of grievance resolutions so often favor the management in power: It costs money to hire professional representation. However, if an employee enlists legal counsel, he might as well resign from the company because his grievance negotiations are now on an equal footing with management, and management does not favor being put at any disadvantage in such disputes. So what at first glance is promoted as an employee perk is really a tool to control the thoughts and actions of a company's workers.

Getting Rid of People

In times of an economic downturn in the fortunes of a company, the quickest solution is to shed employees as rapidly as possible and to use euphemisms to disguise what is really happening. Terms like *rightsizing, downsizing, shifting workers,* and *employee transfers* are all meant to soften the impact. Now, transferring employees looks OK on the surface, but when the transfer is from a sunbelt climate to a state bordering Canada, you begin to wonder how many employees will even consider it. People eligible for retirement probably will not go, people who can get an equivalent job locally probably will not go, and people who will not get an equivalent position at the new location probably will not go. So the net result is that employees leave the company, and the desired objective (getting rid of people) is met with little adverse publicity. Companies have even gone so far as to transfer employees to a new site with the official reason of consolidating operations to reduce costs. Then the company does a reverse and offers the transferred employees severance incentives to leave the company once they become settled at the new location. Again, this trick is meant to maintain the company's image as a good corporate citizen in the news media, while the hidden agenda was to get rid of people one way or another.

Another favorite word used by companies to shed employees is *reorganize.* In today's world, one meaning of this word is to redefine job responsibilities such that only a portion of the company's present employees will qualify for the available jobs. Some companies even make workers periodically re-apply for the remaining jobs to create the perception of fairness. In fact this technique is used to re-evaluate people with an eye on getting rid of higher-salaried people while keeping less-compensated workers. Relying on the duplication-of-function reason, companies often declare a worker surplus and ask some of them to find jobs elsewhere in the company. Normally, looking for such jobs only works for people who have networked contacts. Failing to secure jobs within a reasonable amount of time may tempt workers to volunteer to take severance packages, which, by the way, the company can decrease over time. Meanwhile, the company maintains its image of respecting the individual employee and doing everything possible to avoid layoffs.

For many years, changing the retirement plan has been the tool of companies wishing to get rid of older, retirement-eligible workers. When this occurs, first the company will announce that workers retiring after a particular date will pay more for their medical benefits than workers who elect to retire before that date. This is followed by capping the individual worker's employment years used in calculating retirement pay to a total, such as thirty years. This action almost always guarantees an exodus of older workers. In fact management predicts the number of departing employees that each *negative incentive* will cause.

Still more incentives are used by companies to hasten employees' departure into retirement. Another fine tuning of retirees' medical benefits after a certain date will reduce or even eliminate the company's contribution for insurance to cover the cost differential between Medicare and the actual medical cost incurred. Direct monetary incentives for workers to leave are also offered, with the unspoken caveat that it may be the last time such incentives will be offered so employees had better take it while they can. These are but a few of the tactics that companies employ every day, and most are perfectly legal. In fact the laws that govern such practices continually favor corporations because, after all, don't corporations keep people off the public dole?

A large corporation has various mechanisms that it invokes to decrease its work force while maintaining the semblance of a benevolent employer. Remember that ethics and legality are two different things. When profits and financial survival are at stake, past employment assurances of a company mean nothing unless they are legally enforceable. Learn to read the signs of a corporation that is beginning to compromise its culture for the sake of the bottom line in its annual report.

The Slanted Perception of Veteran Workers

All individuals age with the passing of time. Even star employees are not immune to this process. However, characteristics such as leadership, energy, daring, and inventiveness are somehow associated with people in their twenties and thirties. Of course culture, advertising, and Hollywood all play a great part in these perceived truths. Subconsciously, management views older workers as lacking in one or more attributes needed to move an enterprise into the next decade of product development and a resultant growth. This perception may occur because seasoned individuals tend to dismiss all the hoopla associated with starting something new by asking tough questions about the proposed endeavor. However, the act of questioning the direction determined by management usually relegates these mature doubters to minor roles. The fact that the doubters have been there before and recognize the symptoms of a turkey doesn't influence management to listen to their critiques. Instead, younger individuals lacking the test of experience may commit to halfway-thought-out endeavors without really knowing what they have committed to do.

Because younger workers have nothing to lose by being daring, many will take chances on most anything. These inexperienced leaders pick up the latest jargon such as *quality driven, zero defects, state of the art,* and *world class* to lend credibility to their decision to support any project in which they were given a leading role. At this juncture, the older worker may find himself reporting to a young energetic, dynamic manager whom he believes is totally out of touch with reality.

Some companies even group senior disgruntled workers in the same department so they can be ranked against each other and thus receive lower performance rankings and raises. What to do? The most common outs for the seasoned veteran are to simply:

- ✧ Wait for the project to get killed by its own dead weight.
- ✧ Ask to transfer to another project. (However, most of the time, management takes action against such outspoken employees by giving them nebulous assignments, hoping that boredom forces the workers to make a rash decision like quitting.)
- ✧ Quit the company and find another job. This choice is becoming more and more viable in today's world of minimal permanent-worker staffs. Companies shed employees at the drop of a hat to boost the bottom line, so act accordingly. Besides, with 401(k) plans people are no longer tied to a single company, and employees can take their pensions with them.
- ✧ Try to fix the failings of the project within the system. This is by far the most agonizing choice when the people in power think they have all the answers. They may also think older workers tend to always point out problems. But instead of practicing unquestioning loyalty, seasoned individuals need answers to their doubts before jumping into something that will demand extra hours of work both on weekdays and weekends.

Subtle Tactics Companies Use on Their Employees

Employee benefits is one area that a company can tamper with without any interference from government. After all, what the company giveth, the company can taketh away. Take the accrued vacation pay an employee receives from her employer when she retires. Never mind that no interest is paid on the vacation money that was effectively kept in escrow, but such unused vacation pay also does not count toward service time and thus is not included in the calculation of her retirement pay.

Next let's look at the illusion created when a company says it is increasing its contribution to your tax-deferred savings account. It accompanies such an announcement with much fanfare. However, a close look reveals that the increase only applies if you are already making significant contributions to your tax-deferred savings account. To the worker who needs all his paycheck to meet current expenses, the perceived benefits enhancement has zero effect. Only people at the higher ranges of the compensation ladder can take advantage of this new policy. So what was hailed as a benevolent act by the company turns out to be tacitly restricted to higher-paid workers. Now that the company has all workers thinking they will gain from this new perk, a corporation will simultaneously and quietly eliminate some other benefit (paid to every employee) that was costing the company significantly more than the new publicized enhancement will. So the net of the benefit changes will actually decrease costs to the company while creating the illusion that employees will get an increase in their retirement packages.

Relocating to advance your career has been a path to upward job mobility since the early twentieth century. In the past, companies would reimburse you for most all expenses related to the move. This would include meals, hotel, moving van, travel to the new location, and so on. Recent calculations by the corporate bean counters determined that, for non-executives, allocating a fixed sum of money for moving is less costly than paying for the actual expenses incurred. The effect on employees is to try and move as inexpensively as possible. This may include driving to the new location, renting a drive-it-yourself van, and staying with relatives. Companies instituting double standards that separate executive moves from regular employee moves do so quietly because in many cases this act is a direct reversal of prior stated policy, which is supposed to treat everyone equally. You see, a company can say it still pays for all an employee's moving expenses but fail to effectively communicate the fact that this type of reimbursement is limited and granted at the discretion of the company. This leaves room for interpreting who gets the full move and who doesn't. Guess what! Most of the employee-initiated moves will probably be paid by the fixed-fee plan if at all.

In addition, corporations used to value employees who worked for twenty-five years or more. Now the vogue in this regard is to entice (via a severance package or other forms of coercion) older workers to leave the business because:

- ↪ Companies believe that younger workers can be molded into the kind of employee that managers believe are needed. Age breeds cynicism and a show-me attitude. Youth is innocent of the ways of corporate life, and the company takes advantage of this characteristic.
- ↪ Benefits (for example, health and life insurance) for older employees cost more than for younger workers.
- ↪ Younger workers are usually more willing to work overtime. For many, family responsibilities take a backseat to the company's wishes.
- ↪ Older workers openly express their priorities, like "God, then country, then family, then company." This belief detracts from the absolute loyalty demanded by some of today's companies. Younger workers are more likely to subjugate their beliefs to the will of the company.
- ↪ Younger workers do not question an irrational direction given by management as openly as older workers do. This lessens or eliminates the immediate friction between managers and workers but causes problems later when projects fail because of poor analysis, design, schedules, business cases, and so on.
- ↪ Younger workers make less money for performing similar jobs.
- ↪ Younger workers are perceived as the source of new ideas, while management often views the suggestions and contributions of its more-experienced employees as outdated.

Companies hail their medical coverage as one of an employee's greatest benefits. Although this claim may have been valid in times past, companies are increasingly shifting the burden of medical costs directly to the employee. And the worker's share of this only increases with the passage of time. Most employees have never seen it decrease. You don't really know the extent of your medical coverage until you try to use it. Only then might you discover that, even when the medical plan's written documents indicate the company covers certain illnesses at 100 percent, the fine print reveals some exceptions. For example, side effect medications for the illness may not qualify for the 100 percent coverage. And guess what—the side effect medications are among the most expensive. Even more distressing is the fact that medical insurers' administrators often know less about the medical coverage than you do. If you ask for an itemized list of medications that are covered fully, you may be told that no such list exists because it changes every day. How ridiculous! How can a medical plan be administered when reimbursement depends on whom you communicate with on any given day?

Being so treated, you might suspect that government agencies exist to guard against such abuses. In fact government brochures encourage individuals to register complaints about suspected ill treatment. However, after filing such a complaint, you may discover that the medical plan of the company does not fall under government (state or federal) jurisdiction because it is private to the company. How convenient. Even hospital costs like pain medication offer ways for insurers to shift their cost to the individual. For example, although the pain medication itself may be covered, the *management of the pain medication* may be only partially covered. The definition of *pain management* remains elusive, but you must admit that this term sounds impressive. So beware of company propaganda extolling the virtues of any benefit package. They tell you one thing to disarm your scrutiny (like your medical benefits grow along with your time of service), but the small print can say your employment is terminated if any illness costs more than your earned medical benefits.

More About Benefit Illusions

As an enticement to work for particular companies, what seem like excellent benefits are offered to prospective employees. However, only after you try to use these benefits do you become aware of their shortcomings. One touted benefit is the right to accrue vacation whenever the needs of the business dictate that taking your vacation would not be in the best interests of the company. So, you don't actually lose vacation at this point, but you must take it at the convenience of the company. Usually, a company invokes this right whenever customer commitments are in danger of being compromised and your job contributions are needed to help correct the situation. So you end up working during the time you thought you would be on vacation. Sound fair? Read on. This kind gesture on your part may be met with a subsequent company mandate that you must take all or a portion of your vacation during certain years—and if you don't take your vacation, you will lose it.

Taking your vacation even during normal conditions invites overtime both before and after your vacation because, as some skilled workers realize, no one is performing your job in your absence. So you end up working long hours immediately before and after your vacation so you can be absent from work. Add your normal earned vacation for a given year to the must-take accrued vacation, and you can see that the mere thought of taking all this time off actually causes the employee undue stress.

Next, there is the highly touted company contribution to tax-deferred compensation—it may be like a 401(k) plan. Companies say they will match an employee's contribution to a tax-deferred savings plan up to a certain percentage (say half of the first 6 percent of your annual salary). What they don't tell you up front is that if the percentage you contribute to the plan meets some maximum amount before the company's portion is reached, you lose the remainder of the company's contribution. Could a company automatically adjust its payroll deduction process to see that this doesn't happen? Sure, but companies do not always play fair, especially when money is involved. Can companies do this? Sure, and as you become more astute you will realize that management can change the rules of the game at any time. In fact a company can terminate any of its benefit plans in whole or in part. The seasoned employee begins to realize that no benefit is guaranteed. If a benefit plan becomes weak financially over time, you will discover that a provision has already been made to distribute any remaining assets according to a distribution priority determined by the company. In today's work environment, the trend is for employees to change jobs frequently because companies no longer value loyalty or longevity. So employees may be left out in the cold because they did not attain vested-right status in a company's benefit plan.

Medical benefits have been getting a lot of attention recently because these costs are accelerating at a rapid pace. However, in a company-funded medical plan, adequate or even total coverage is alluded to, when in fact often only a portion of medical costs will be paid by the company's insurance plan. Whether you get the proper reimbursement or not depends on the individual who processes your claim. You may even find that the corporation has contracted with another insurance company to administer the plan. While trying to get a resolution to a known error or even asking a question, you will often be "bounced around" from insurer to administrator ad nauseam. In a dispute, the funding and administrating companies will each claim it is the other's fault, but you ultimately will be stuck with resolving the problem. Finally you will end up resolving the problem and educating each company about the details of the medical plan. Unbelievable but true! Therefore, know your own benefit plan instead of blindly trusting the medical insurers to do their jobs.

Some Compensation Illusions

In times of poor profit performance and employee defection to opportunities at other companies, large businesses like to spread the illusion that they offer similar benefits as do small firms. For example, employees are told they can earn bonus money (also known as variable pay) based on how well their products do in the marketplace. (Note that this expected bonus is calculated as part of an employee's total income.) So the company then limits the individual's guaranteed salary, saying that the bonus money will more than make up the difference.

The pay reduction is accomplished in a variety of subtle ways. The most obvious one is that raises are suspended for the fixed part of your compensation. This tactic not only buys the company time, but management can now blame your lack of income directly on you. Management may have directed you in what products to make, when to market the products, and how to price them, but it becomes your own fault that your products were not readily accepted in the marketplace, and management comes out clean because the "opportunity" was there. The true objective in times of lackluster company profit performance is to reduce the company's salary expense because bonus money is high risk. Meanwhile, managers' stock options continue because it appears as if they are keeping fixed costs to a minimum. This ruse achieves the effect wanted by the company (reduced salary expenses, reduced employee defection, and the pretense of a small company atmosphere).

On another note, in times of extended overtime lower-ranking employees usually bear the brunt of unrealistic schedules and so tend to work long and demanding hours. Caught up in the enthusiasm of a project in which they believe, employees often disregard their personal lives for the good of the product. But this can become detrimental to their careers, as I shall demonstrate. As weeks extend into months and months into years, a favorite company technique is to suddenly promote an employee to *exempt* status. At first glance this seems to be a good thing. But on further inspection, it rapidly becomes apparent that the term *exempt* means "exempt from being paid overtime." Your work hours do not diminish when you become exempt. Soon individuals become smart, and they often turn down promotions because it means a decrease in compensation. The danger in this strategy is that such an individual becomes tagged with the reputation of not being a company person or not being part of the team. Management fails to recognize humankind's basic belief in getting a fair day's pay for a fair day's work. This belief may doom an individual to the lower ranks of a company for years.

Management's Fostering of the Critical Resource Shortage Phenomenon

Every day the public is bombarded with the perceived shortage of domestic workers possessing critical skills in the professional ranks. This reasoning is used by management to hire thousands and thousands of "green-card workers" from such far-off places as India, China, and other places an ocean away from California. Most important is the fact that these countries have a low wage scale. It is unusual to hear of corporate workers being imported into the United States from European nations because the workers from these places have a high wage rate and a high standard of living compared with workers from the Orient. These foreign workers are mostly young and in their twenties, so they have little or no experience. Even though they often lack the proper job background, management says it can train them in no time at all. After all, educated individuals are used to learning. But there are young, educated people in this country too, and they are not given the same job opportunities!

Still the importation of cheap professional workers persists. Why? Corporate America is profit-hungry and will use any excuse to keep the cost of doing business as low as possible. This is not a bad goal if it is not the only one. However, the public is fed rhetoric that makes potential U.S. workers believe that somehow they are at fault. Hiring foreign workers fosters the illusion that plenty of jobs exist—if only prospective employees in this country possessed the right skills. The public is therefore led to believe that large corporations are good corporate citizens that provide jobs to the masses.

Another benefit for companies that hire non-citizens is that young, foreign employees tend to work long hours because the workplace offers a familiar haven in a land where the culture can be so different. In a strange country, lack of a family/friend support system makes working that much more tolerable. A closer look at industry groups reveals that the critical resource phenomenon is closely related to working long hours. Take the software industry as an example. Thousands and thousands of unemployed older workers possess skills that are easily extrapolated into any program development environment. Yet this senior group continues to have a difficult time securing employment in their chosen career field. The work force in the software industry continues to be populated by young workers. Why? Companies need employees who possess the necessary background (or can be easily trained) AND who are willing to work sixty to eighty hours per week for extended periods of time WITHOUT any overtime compensation.

Only work-innocent people in their early careers are taken in by this ploy. They are eager to work because, in college, they labored long hours and didn't get paid a nickel. Soon, however, this enthusiasm wears thin. Marriage, families, and a life outside work begin to take on more and more relevance. So the cycle continues. Opportunities are given to the young. However, someday young workers become old workers.

Conclusion

Today's corporations treat their work forces as inanimate objects, like pencils, desks, or paper clips. The attitude seems to be to pay the least for the most. Unfortunately, this biggest-bang-for-the-buck philosophy has been elevated into the ranks of the breathing people resource. Such nonsense has effected a change in culture for many companies. Can this last? Well, stay tuned because workers have adopted their own enlightened attitude in this new corporate world by espousing a disposition that says, "Give the least for the most." Will this new math of the corporate world survive? Who wins in the end? Should it be a game with winners and losers? An attitude of times past fostered the notion that companies should be in partnership with their employees. There is no motivator like personal involvement.

Closing Remarks

~ of ~

Either Use Your Noggin or Take a Floggin'

Just as it is comforting to discover a word in the dictionary that describes an individual or circumstance that has puzzled you, the scenarios in this book regarding life in a large corporation are meant to provide comfort regarding day-to-day work experiences.

The fact that all these experiences appear in this book means that someone else has already encountered individuals or situations that you may be experiencing for the first time. So you are not alone. If you can relate to the topics discussed in this book, then view your workday with a touch of humor and take satisfaction in the realization that, after all, jobs exist to obtain money so you can enjoy life outside the workplace.

Index

About the Author

T. R. Edel compiled his extensive knowledge of workplace personalities and situations during his 35 years in the computer industry. Before his retirement in June 1996, he was a senior programmer. He lives in Mesa, Arizona.